NEW
PRICE ONE SHILLING

MAP & GUIDE
TO
...TOGLE

FROM
...STEELE & SON
...EST AUTHORITIES

& ALL RAILWAY BOOKSTALLS

AS...
COAC...

...ING CONNECTING
...RVICES WITH
...TOGLE AND THE
...T COAST OF
...COTLAND

...ly from
...chentogle

...COACHES LTD
...OUNDEE - ABERDEEN -
...UCHENTOGLE

VIMT...
BOO...
For Scho...

KNOWL...
IS POW...

This is the property...

......

PRESENTED BY THE PROPRIE...
VIM T...

B.C.M./VIMTO. ALL RIGHTS RESERVED

MAW'S FIRST SIGHT O' HER HAME FAE HAME –
– THE BUT AN' BEN

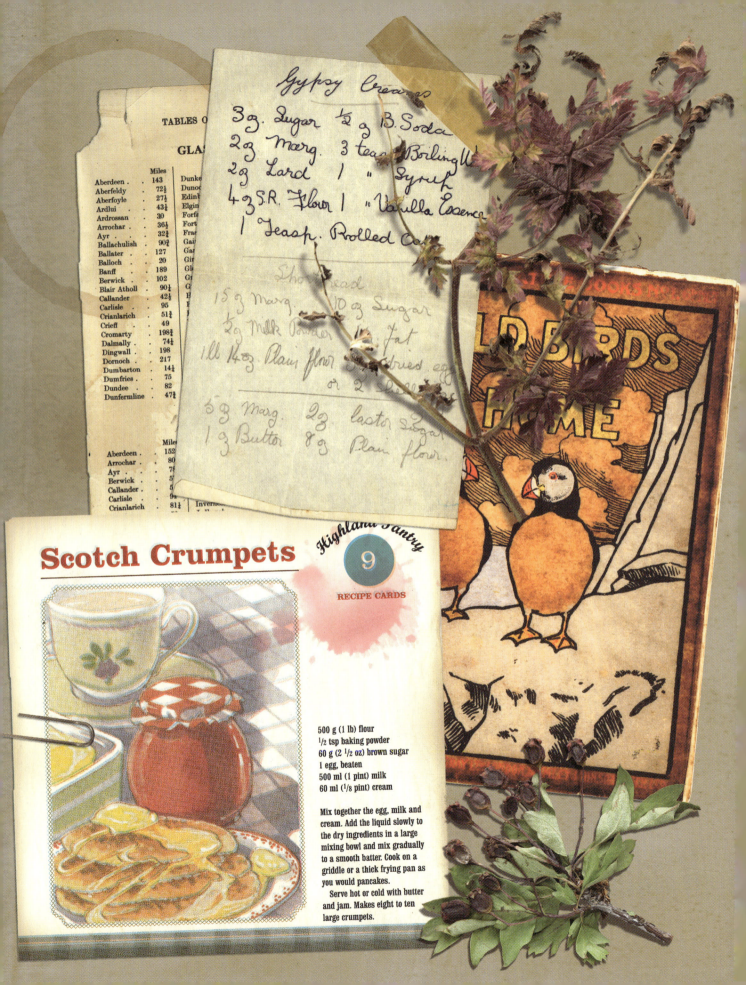

Gypsy Creams

3 g. Sugar   ½ g B. Soda
2 g. Marg.   3 teasp. Boiling W...
2 g Lard   1 "   Syrup
4 g S.R. Flour 1 " Vanilla Essence
1 Teasp. Rolled Oa...

Shortbread

15 g Marg.   10 oz Sugar
½ g Milk Powder ... fat
1 lb 14 oz. Plain flour ... dried egg
                 or 2 ...

5 g Marg.   2 g Castor Sugar
1 g Butter   8 g Plain flour.

LD BIRDS
H ME

Scotch Crumpets

Highland Pantry

9

RECIPE CARDS

500 g (1 lb) flour
½ tsp baking powder
60 g (2 ½ oz) brown sugar
1 egg, beaten
500 ml (1 pint) milk
60 ml (⅛ pint) cream

Mix together the egg, milk and
cream. Add the liquid slowly to
the dry ingredients in a large
mixing bowl and mix gradually
to a smooth batter. Cook on a
griddle or a thick frying pan as
you would pancakes.

Serve hot or cold with butter
and jam. Makes eight to ten
large crumpets.

No' tae be removed fae the But an' Ben!

The But an' Ben Cookbook

Can we go to Tenerife next year?

Published 2008 by Waverley Books, an imprint of Geddes & Grosset Ltd.
David Dale House, New Lanark, Scotland, ML11 9DJ.

Design, layout, and text copyright © 2008 Waverley Books and
D.C. Thomson & Co. Ltd.

Devised by Ron Grosset.
Text and layout by Eleanor Abraham.
Illustrations by Hugo Breingan.
Cover, endpapers and additional design
  and illustrations by Mark Mechan.
Cover embroidery by Moira Anne
  Dickson and Margaret Cowan.

Production: Craig Brown.
Editors: Eleanor Abraham, Penny
  Grearson.
Cookery consultant: Louise Sinclair.
Broons consultant: David Donaldson.
Index: Margaret Christie.
Publishers: Mike Miller and Ron Grosset.

Maw Broon, The Broons logo and supporting characters appear courtesy of,
and are copyright © 2008 D.C. Thomson & Co. Ltd.
Cartoon strips and selected items are from the Sunday Post and People's
Friend archive and are courtesy of D.C. Thomson & Co. Ltd.

Conditions of Sale
This book is sold with the condition that it will not, by way of trade or
otherwise, be re-sold, hired out, lent, or otherwise distributed or circulated
in any form or style of binding or cover other than that in which it is
published and without the same condition being imposed on the subsequent
purchaser.

Maw and the publisher canna be held responsible for any recipes that go wrang
or if ye dinna follow the instructions right or dinna pay attention to modern food
hygiene rules. An we're warning you, dinna go picking and eating wild food that
you dinna recognise. Take a tellin'!

ISBN 13 : 978-1-902407-61-6

Printed and bound in the EU

3 4 5 6 7 8 9 10

QUALITY FAMILY HOTEL

AUCHENTOGLE
COUNTRY HOUSE HOTEL

Telephone: Auchentogle 662

If things go
pear-shaped ye
can aye book ^
  in here |
IMPORTINT bit
  ←

The rights of Gran'maw Broon and Maw Broon tae be identified as authors of this work
The Bero® Home Recipes Book appears by permission of
Premiere Foods Group Limited.
Shakespeare Flyreel ® leaflet appears by permission of
the Shakespeare company.
Barlow's map of Auchentogle is an adaptation of a
Bartholomew® Map and is adapted and reproduced by
permission of Collins Maps and Atlases, HarperCollins.
The Guide to National Insurance and National Identity
Card are Crown Copyright.
The New Vimto Book for Scholars, first published in
1949, is provided by Vimto Soft Drinks (1908-2008).
Vimto® is a registered trademark of Nichols PLC.
Aitken's Bakery bag appears with permission of the Aitken
family.

Acknowledgements

Museum tickets, maps and NTS membership
cards appear courtesy of the National Trust for
Scotland.

With thanks to David Donaldson,
Alex Gray, Louise Sinclair, Margaret
Christie, Shonaig Macpherson, Margaret
Cowan, Eileen and Nicky Smith,
Liz Small, Bea Neilson,
Frances O'Brien, Jean Brownlee,
Charlotte McCrone

We have made every effort to contact the
copyright holders of material reproduced in this
book. If we have made any omissions please
contact us at: David Dale House, New Lanark,
Scotland, ML11 9DJ

Dear Family

This is the But an' Ben Cookbook. It is tae be kept at the But an' Ben, in the dresser drawer.

We're no' always a' here at the same time — although that's when it's the maist fun — so when I'm no' here I want tae know that you lot know how tae feed yersels and look efter the hoose. There should be a'thing in here that ye need tae know aboot staying at and cooking in oor wee hame-fae-hame.

If ye want tae add onything o' yer ain — maps, addresses, guid walks, directions, recipes, pictures — stick them in here so that ithers can get the use o' them and we can aye look back an mind the braw times we've had at oor wee holiday hoose.

I've written doon some guid recipes that ye can mak' on the But an' Ben cooker (even though it's a wee bitty temperamental) and some guid recipes for using the things ye can pick wild or buy here. Get yer eggs, milk, an' cheese frae Farmer Gray an' there's guid places for the berry pickin' an' tattie howkin'.

The But an' Ben Rules:

1. Keep a tidy hoose!: Make yer ain bed an' tidy up efter yersel. The But an' Ben is too wee for there tae be a guddle!

   Tak' the rubbish oot an' pit it at the fit o' the lane.

2. Fires: Dinna leave a fire burning in the grate withoot the fireguard being up, an' dinna leave it burning when ye leave for Glebe Street.

   Dinna leave that barbecue burning without someone tae watch it an' mak' sure the bairns are no' allowed anywhere near it.

   If the logs look low before you leave, get some mair. If I arrive an' there's nae wood left for my fire, there'll be trouble!

3. Walks: If ye go for a walk or a hike leave a note of whaur ye're going. Then

4

if ye fall doon a big ditch we'll ken whaur tae start lookin'!

Leave dirty boots at the door, an' mind an' clean them yersel.

Leave the gates as ye find them when ye go a walk — follow the country code now!

4. Picnics: Tak a' yer rubbish hame wi' ye if ye go a picnic.

A' the picnic flasks an' tubs are tae be washed afore they are put by.

5. Fishing: Look efter the fishing stuff an' put it by each time ye use it.

6. Foraging: Dinna ever eat onything ye dinna recognise!!

7. When ye leave: Lock up after yersel' an' check the windaes are a' shut.

Let Farmer Gray know ye're going if ye see him (he'll keep an eye on the place).

8. Nae dirty dishes tae be left when ye go!!

9. Dinna miss the bus! The timetable is in the book.

10. Have fun!

Lots of love,

Maw

When horace went fishing all he caught was an auld boot

Naw, he caught the cold tae.

Oven temperatures

The But an' Ben cooker is a bit temperamental and still has temperatures in fahrenheit so here's a wee translation

Very Slow	= 225–275°F	110–140°C	gas mark ½ – 1
Slow	= 300°F	150°C	gas mark 2
Slow Moderate	= 325°F	160°C	gas mark 3
Moderate	= 350°F	180°C	gas mark 4
Quick	= 375°F	190°C	gas mark 5
Moderately Hot	= 400°F	200°C	gas mark 6
Hot	= 425–450°F	220–230°C	gas mark 7–8
Very Hot	= 480–500°F	240–260°C	gas mark 9

Roasting Meat

Moderate oven, 350°F, 180°C, gas mark 4 to 5:

Chicken	20 minutes per lb (45 per kg) plus 20 minutes
Beef Rare	20 minutes per lb (45 per kg) plus 20 minutes
Beef Medium	25 minutes per lb (55 per kg) plus 20 minutes
Beef Well-done	30 minutes per lb (66 per kg) plus 30 mins
Pork Medium	30 minutes per lb (66 per kg) plus 30 minutes
Pork Well-done	35 minutes per lb (77 per kg) plus 35 minutes
Lamb Medium	25 minutes per lb (55 per kg) plus 25 mins at 350°F
Lamb Well-done	30 minutes per lb (66 per kg) plus 30 mins at 350°F
Mutton	40-45 minutes per lb (88 to 99 per kg) at 350°F
or	First 15 minutes at 500°F (250°C) then 25-30 minutes per lb (55-66 per kg) at 350°F
Venison	15-20 minutes per lb (33-44 per kg)

Contents

Temperatures

Gas Mark	°F	°C
	32	0
	50	10
	100	40
	122	50
	212	100
1	275	140
2	300	150
3	325	160
4	350	180
5	375	190
6	400	200
7	425	220
8	450	230
9	475	250

Liquid Measures

Unit		fl oz	ml
teaspoon	1/3 tbsp.	1/5 fl oz	5 ml
dessertspoon	2 tsps	2/5 fl oz	10 ml
tablespoon	3 tsps.	3/5 fl oz	15 ml
cup	scant 1/2 pt.	8 fl oz	225 ml
breakfastcup	1/2 pt.	10 fl oz	285 ml
fluid ounce	2 tbsps	1/20 pint	28 ml
1 pint	2 cups	20 fl oz	570 ml
gill	1/4 pint	5 fl oz	140 ml
quart	2 pints	40 fl oz	1136 ml
1/2 pint	1 cup	10 fl oz	285 ml
1/4 pint	1/2 cup	5 fl oz	115 ml
2 pints	1 quart	40 fl oz	1136 ml
1 litre	4 1/2 cups scant 2 pts		1000 ml
gallon	4 quarts	8 pt	4560 ml

Dry Weights

Imperial	Metric (exact)	Metric (1oz=25g)
1/8 oz	3.5 g	3 g
1/4 oz	7 g	6.25 g
1/2 oz	14 g	12.5 g
1 oz	28 g	25 g
2 oz	57 g	50 g
3 oz	85 g	75 g
4 oz	113 g	100 g
5 oz	141 g	125 g
6 oz	170 g	150 g
7 oz	198 g	175 g
8 oz	226 g	200 g
9 oz	255 g	225 g
10 oz	283 g	250 g
11 oz	312 g	275 g
12 oz	340 g	300 g
13 oz	368 g	325 g
14 oz	396 g	350 g
15 oz	425 g	375 g
1 lb	453 g	400 g
1 1/2 lb	680 g	600 g
2 lbs	900 g	800 g
2 1/2 lb	1134 g	1 kg
2.3 lb	1 kg	1000 g

Measurements

Inches	Centimetres/Millimetres
1/8	3 mm
1/4	6 mm
2/5 (0.39)	1 cm
1/2	1.3 cm
3/4	1.9 cm
1	2.54 cm
2	5 cm
3	7.6 cm
4	10 cm
5	12.7 cm
6	15.2 cm
7	17.8 cm
8	20.3 cm
9	22.8 cm
10	25.4 cm
11	28 cm
12	30.5 cm

Picnics
an' food for on the move

Choose sandwich fillings that dinna mah' yer breid a' soggy — but ye can use lettuce leaves tae keep the moisture in, and a guid layer o' butter will help tae. Boiled eggs, chicken legs, salad boxes and a flask o' soup are a' guid things tae tah'. Tah' the big broon case and the big tartan case, or, if we hae visitors, use the fancy hamper Auntie Betty sent us.

Falkland

JACOBUS V

MEMBERS' TICKET

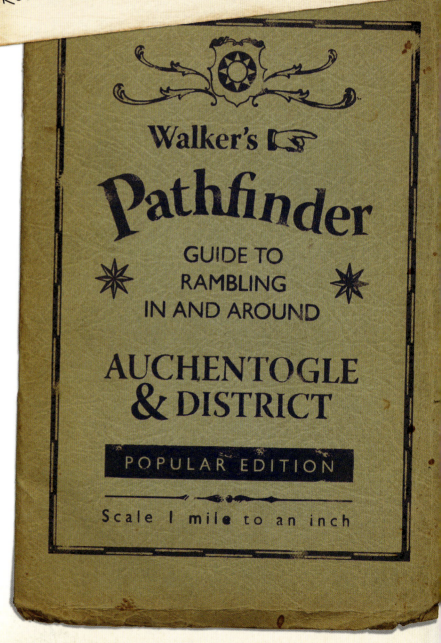

Things I tak' tae the But an' Ben, by Joe

Tinnies
Swiss army knife
Walking boots
My good socks
Rucksack

My piece box
Kendal Mint Cake
Guide to the Pubs of Scotland
Commando comic

Walker's

Pathfinder

GUIDE TO
RAMBLING
IN AND AROUND

AUCHENTOGLE & DISTRICT

POPULAR EDITION

Scale 1 mile to an inch

Hard-Boiled Eggs

1 Dinna boil straight fae the fridge.

2 Use a timer.

3 Dinna use an ower big pot.

4 Simmer them, dinna boil.

5 Hard boiled eggs for picnics should be cooled completely, immediately after cooking, or the yolks will get yon black rings roon them. Plunge into cold water and leave for aboot 10 minutes.

6 For pinics: tak' wee twists o' salt in grease-proof paper or foil tae sprinkle on eggs.

Add the eggs tae a pan o' cold water. Bring tae the boil. The second ye see the water boil, start the timer an' turn the heat doon tae a simmer.

For hard-boiled wi' slightly moist yolk, simmer for 6 minutes.

For completely hard-boiled eggs, simmer for 7 minutes.

See page 137 for all the ways to cook a boiled egg. A runny yolk for me, Maw. I wa o' them wi' toast sodjers!

Things I tak' tae the But an' Ben, by Maw

Knitting patterns

Cross-stitch and embroidery

The People's Friend

Flasks

Jeely jaurs for jam makin'

Lunch boxes and tinnies

The messages:

    tea bags

    coffee

    tinned meat

    loaf

    ju-jubes

Things We Tak Tae The BUT an' Ben bY The TWin'

Pens pencils paper

fishing nets

bucket and spade

fishing Tackle

The Beano

The DanDY

Plastic spiders

Wind-up mouse

Whoopee cushion

Things I tak' tae the But an' Ben, by Horace

Net

Jam jars

Magnifying glass

Notebook

Pencils

Charcoal

Drawing pad

Paints

Observer Book of Birds

Observer Book of Wild Flowers

Book of Wild Food

Midge repellent

Poetry Book

Things I tak' tae the But an' Ben, by Granpaw

Gardening notebook

Wine-making notebook

A wee dram

My baccy and my second-best pipe

Granny sookers

My Summer bunnet

Bucket and spade

Things the Bairn taks tae the But an' Ben:

Her dolly

Her dolly's pal

Her dolly's pram

Bucket and spade

12

Layered Loaf

Get the loaf fae Browning's — lovely and crusty!

This is a handy way tae transport enough sandwiches fir a'body in the one bundle — jist mind tae tak the bread knife wi' ye or ye'll a' be tearing lumps oot o' the loaf wi' yer haunds!

1 round farmhouse crusty loaf
2 cooked chicken breasts, sliced thinly
Lettuce leaves (or wild watercress, sorrel, rocket an' young dandelion leaves)
Tomatoes (deseeded), sliced
Cucumber, sliced
Butter (or mayonnaise or salad cream)
Salt an' pepper

Slice the top aff the loaf an' butter it. Hollow oot maist o' the loaf (keep this for breadcrumbs for yer burgers). Butter the inside. Layer the salad an' chicken inside till it's stappit fu' (start an' finish wi' lettuce an' season the layers). Place top back on. Chill overnight in the fridge, wrapped in foil an' wi' a weighted breadboard on top. Tak' on picnics whole, an' slice in wedges when ready tae eat.

13

Pieces

These is the only akseptabil sandwiches in oor oppinyins

Chese Pieces

2 slices plain bread
BUTTER
Pickel
Chese (not too chesey chese)

Spred bread with butter. Put not too chesey chese between slices. Spread with pickel. Cut in half (not triangles!!!!). For day trips wrap in the paper wrapper aff the plain loaf. Also delicious eaten while sitting on the back step so you don't need a plate.

Piece an Jam

1 slice Pan Bread
BUTTER
Jam

Spred one slice of pan bread with butter. Spred butter with Jam.

This is the crewshal part: FOLD the bread over. DO NOT CUT! Cutting lets oot the flavour. Also can be eaten on the back doorstep for that extra je ne say pah.

Bong appeteet!

We're going looking for Tadpoles today!

Mince Sandwiches

A fusion o' French an' Scottish cuisine!? I like tae use lamb mince an' cook it quite brown. The Americans would ca' this a Sloppy Joe. Awfy tasty. Jist like oor ain Joe!

1lb lean lamb mince
2 onions, chopped
Salt an' pepper
3 wee baguette rolls or round crusty
      rolls
Butter
Strong-tasting salad leaves like rocket

Brown the mince thoroughly in its ain fat — takes approximately 20 minutes. Add the onions and cook to soften them for aboot another 10 minutes. Season. Drain aff all the fat, an' leave it tae cool. Slice open the baguettes an' tak' oot some o' the middle. Butter. Fill wi' salad leaves an' the mince, an' wrap in foil an' chill for nae mair than an hour or twa. Eat that day.

Write what ye want in your picnic pieces here—

Granpaw: Strong cheese wi' beetroot chutney

Paw: Boiled ham an' mustard

Maw: Egg an' cress

Hen: Sausages an' broon sauce

Joe: Bacon an' broon sauce

Maggie: Lemon curd

Daphne: Corned beef an' tomato

Ae Twin: STRAWBERRY Jam

Ither Twin: Chese (not too chesey)

Horace: Banana

The Bairn: Jeely

Liver Paté

$^{1}/_{2}$ lb of calf or lamb's liver
Sprig of thyme and a bay leaf
2 ozs bacon
Dessertspoonful cream

Cut the bacon into small pieces, fry it in a pan to let out as much fat as possible, add the liver and herbs, and cook for about te minutes. Remove the herbs, chop finely then sieve the mixtur and add the cream. Press firmly into a small pot.

Toast some thick white bread and let it cool. Spread with th paté and with cranberry or rowan jelly.

Two Kinds of Scotch Eggs

Scotch Egg

2 hard-boiled eggs
3 sausages
Dried breadcrumbs

Remove skin from the sausages, flour the hands, and make the meat into two balls. Mould around the eggs.

Dip this in beaten egg and breadcrumbs and fry in deep fat till the sausage is thoroughly cooked.

Vegetarian Scotch Egg

One beaten egg
4 oz breadcrumbs
1 oz melted butter
Pepper and salt to taste
One teaspoonful mixed herbs
One teaspoonful chopped parsley
2 hard-boiled eggs
Dried breadcrumbs

Mix egg, crumbs, butter and seasoning together well, and mould round 2 boiled eggs. Dip in more beaten egg, coat in more breadcrumbs and deep fry till golden brown.

Posh Layered Sandwiches

Very fancy looking for posh veesitors if ye cut the crusts aff. I eat the crusts later anyway, dipped in ma soup!

Thick-sliced brown bread
Thick-sliced white bread
Soft white cream cheese
Thin-sliced, honey-roast ham
Mustard
1 fresh tomato, skinned, seeded and
  very finely chopped
Fresh parsley, chopped

To skin a tomato, cut a cross in its bottom and put in a bowl. Pour boiling water over and leave for a few minutes. The skin should then peel away easily.

Layer one: White bread spread wi' cream cheese, topped wi' a layer o' ham, and a scrape o' mustard. Layer two: Brown bread spread on one side wi' cream cheese. Place cheese-side doon on top o' ham. Layer three: Some cream cheese mixed wi' chopped tomato an' chopped parsley, spread on white bread. Place, cheese-side down, on the middle layer o' bread. Cut the crusts aff, an' cut in rectangles. If it's jist us, I dinna bother wi' genteel slices, my boys like big doorstep pieces!

17

Coleslaw

Half a white cabbage, shredded
3 carrots, grated
1 Spanish onion, grated
A pinch of salt
1/2 tsp white pepper (or tae taste)
1/2 tsp black pepper
3 heaped tbsps mayonnaise, (choose the low-fat mayonnaise that is 15 cals a tbsp)

Mix all the above together well for salads and sandwiches. This is quite a peppery coleslaw.

A sweeter alternative is tae miss oot the onion, mayonnaise and pepper and add grated apple and a little cider vinegar.

MAYONNAISE

2 egg yolks
A pinch of salt
A pinch of pepper
1 teaspoon mustard powder
Oil (about 8 fl oz)
1 tbsp white wine vinegar or lemon juice

Set a damp cloth under a fairly large bowl, put in the egg yolks and the salt, pepper and the teaspoon of mustard powder. Add the oil, a little at a time, whisking all the time.

When the mixture is thick and smooth, add, gradually, one tablespoonful white wine vinegar or lemon juice, and beat till the mixture is firm again.

A less fattening mayonnaise

Beat the yolks of three and the whites of two eggs with a teaspoonful dry mustard, a pinch of pepper, salt, and a teaspoon of sugar or granulated sweetener.

Stir in, gradually, about 1/4 pint vinegar, and cook in a bowl above a pan of boiling water, till thick. Bottle when cold.

A mayonnaise that keeps

Keeps for a few months in an airtight jar.

16 fl ozs vinegar
16 fl ozs water
9 level tablespoons caster sugar
1 level tablespoon mustard powder
1/2 teaspoon white pepper
3 tablespoons salt
3 tablespoons butter
3 tablespoons flour
8 whole eggs

Mix sugar, butter, pepper, salt, mustard, and flour into a smooth paste with the water and vinegar, and cook over slow heat till the mixture thickens. Beat the eggs well, pour the mixture slowly over them, stirring all the time; cook in a bowl over a pan of boiling water, and let it become hot but never let it boil. When cold, store in airtight jars.

Steak Pasties

Maks a nice wee change fae jeely pieces.
Cool them an' tak' them wi' ye on a
picnic, wrapped in foil.

1 tsp oil

4 oz potatoes, diced

2 oz carrots, diced

2 oz turnip, diced

1 onion, finely chopped

4 oz lean rump steak, diced

White pepper, pinch o' salt

2 tbsps beef stock

Shortcrust Pastry:

6 oz plain flour an' a pinch o' salt

2 oz butter

2 tbsps water (approx)

Pastry tips:
Sieve the flour. Cut fat into
cubes. Mix using awfy
cold hands (chill them in
cauld water if ye can) rub
the fat into the flour tae
look like breid crumbs. Add
cold water tae mak' a stiff
dough. Roll oot once. Dinna
ower-handle the dough

Preheat the oven tae 425°F. Heat the oil
an' cook the vegetables until they begin
tae soften (10 mins). Mak' the pastry
by rubbing fat into flour an' mixing in
enough water tae bind tae a firm dough.
Divide into four balls. Roll flat.

Brown steak. Mix wi' vegetables,
seasoning an' stock. Add tae centres o'
pastry. Crimp edges o' pastry together in
centre. Bake till golden brown (approx 20
tae 30 minutes).   19

Salad Dressings

A SALAD without a dressing is a sad dish indeed. Dressings entirely improve the flavour of any salad. Ingredients must be of the best quality and freshness and thoroughly mixed, but a good dressing is simplicity itself to achieve.

Olive oil has a strong flavour for some tastes but is by far the best choice for salads. Its nutrients are said to have given the Italians their enviable good health and longevity. It should be kept tightly corked in a cool place.

Other oils, such as sunflower, groundnut, and rapeseed, are less strong tasting and can be substituted if wished.

In very cold weather salad oils may thicken, but fear not, they have not spoiled and are easily made pourable again by warming the bottle in a bowl of hot water.

To buy cheaply is not an economy in the long run for the flavour is much inferior. In addition, the best quality oil is a guarantee of the contents containing the nutrients one needs.

Do not use malt vinegar in a dressing. White wine or cider vinegar tastes much better and so even though it is dearer you will not need to use as much. The proportion of vinegar to oil should be one part vinegar to three or four of oil. Fruit and herb vinegars are very easily made in summer and are useful if you do not have fresh herbs.

All leaves to be coated with dressing must be perfectly dry, or the dressing will not adhere.

Vinaigrette
3 tablespoons olive oil
1 tablespoon red wine vinegar
$^1/_2$ teaspoon salt
$^1/_4$ teaspoon pepper
1 teaspoon of mustard
A pinch of sugar
Crushed clove of garlic to taste

Catalina Dressing
1 teaspoon fine sugar
$^1/_2$ teaspoon mustard
$^1/_2$ teaspoon salt
A pinch of paprika
1 tablespoon lemon juice
1 tablespoon tomato ketchup
1 tablespoon water
5 tablespoons olive oil

Cooked Dressing
Two egg yolks, or one whole egg
1 tablespoon vinegar
$^1/_2$ tablespoon sugar
$^1/_4$ pint boiling water
1 oz flour
$^1/_4$ pint long-life cream
1 teaspoon mustard
1 oz. butter

Melt the butter, add the flour, then the boiling water; stir in the mustard, sugar, and vinegar and mix thoroughly. Boil, allow to cool, add the egg, and lastly the cream. Reheat over a bain marie but do not let it boil, and, when cold, bottle and cork. Refrigerate.

Balsamic Dressing
6 tablespoons olive oil
2 tablespoon balsamic vinegar
$^1/_2$ teaspoon salt
$^1/_4$ teaspoon black pepper
1 teaspoon of mustard
1 teaspoon honey
1 clove garlic crushed

Bacon Salad Dressing
Warm bacon fat
One third of the quantity of fat in warm (not hot) wine vinegar
A pinch of black pepper
A pinch of salt

This is a dressing you could potentially make when camping. Breakfast bacon could provide a warm dressing for a salad of wild leaves gathered for lunch.

Fruit Vinegars in Dressings
Keep these dressings simple, as the vinegar itself will be sweet and tasty. Add a little honey and a little oil and perhaps serve with fruity salads containing crisp lettuce leaves, tinned or fresh peaches, or sliced apples.

Eggs for picnics
Hard boil the number of eggs required (one per person). When cold, take out the yolks, mash them with a little minced ham, butter, and mustard. Fill the hollowed white with the mixture, press the two halves together, wrap the eggs in greased paper and twist the ends to keep them from separating. Put a small twist of paper containing salt in the packet.

Egg an' Cress

Leaves fae wild garlic are braw in egg sandwiches

Ye cannae beat this as a sandwich filling for picnics. It beats fancy sandwiches haunds doon!

4 eggs (hard-boiled)
Mayonnaise
1 tablespoon melted butter
Pepper, salt
Freshly cut cress

Horace likes newts in his

Chop up the eggs by putting them in a big mug (not ane o' my guid china anes!) adding the butter an' seasoning, an' rattling a knife around inside till they're chopped nice an' fine. Add a guid dollop o' mayonnaise an' mix weel. Spread on the bread an' add a guid thick layer o' cress that ye've snipped wi' the kitchen shears. Granpaw will probably be growing a few pots o' cress an' a few o' mustard. If ye want tae mix wi' chopped tomatoes tak' oot the seeds o' the tomatoes first (gie them tae Granpaw for his greenhouse).

Honey Roast Chicken Drumsticks

12 chicken drumsticks (around Auchentogle, the village shop is the place tae get these — whole chickens are best bought, an' nicest, frae McNab's farm)

2 tbsps oil

1 tbsp honey

2 tbsps water

A pinch o' salt

A pinch o' pepper

You can add flavour to a roast whole chicken by doing this right at the end o' the cooking time. Good as a barbie marinade too!

Roast the chicken legs in a roasting pan in a hot oven for around 10 tae 15 minutes. Put the oil, honey, water, salt an' pepper in a jam jar an' shake. (Ye could add, mustard, curry powder, herbs, garlic, wine vinegar, Worcestershire sauce ... anything that takes your fancy!) When the legs start tae broon, tak' oot o' oven an' pour this mixture over them. Gie the pan a richt guid shoogle around tae get them a' coated. Be careful no' tae burn yersel! Ye could aye use a brush or spoon it ower. Roast till the skin o' the drumsticks is crispy an' broon. Cool, an' tak' on a picnic wrapped in foil.

Picnic Checklist

Icepacks for keeping stuff fresh

plasters

sunscreen

Midgie repellent

hats

Insect bite spray

tent

windbreak

dinna forget a jam jar
and net for catchin
baggie minnows

Things I tak' tae the
But an' Ben, by Daphne

Sunglasses
Sunscreen
Comfy shoes
My new hiking socks
Hot water bottle
Rollers
Waterproofs
Turkish delights
"True Love" Weekly

ITISH & MIDLANDS RAILWAY COMPANY

4965

AUCHENTOGLE & THE HIGHLANDS

Information from Auchentogle Station
Telephone Auchentogle 629

Picnic Games
Paddling
Rounders
Wrestling
Egg and spoon Race
Kite flying
Shooting tins wi catties
fitba
fishing
WATER fights!!

24

Salad Leaves

Salad leaves must be gied a richt guid wash, especially if ye've picked wild leaves or anes frae Granpaw's patch. Stick a dash o' salt in the water tae release ony slugs or ither beasties fae the leaves an' wash an' rinse several times.

Dry the leaves. We dinna hae a salad spinner at the But an' Ben — in fact we dinna hae ane at a'! — so I put the leaves in a clean tea towel an' send The Bairn outside tae swing it roon tae get the water oot. She thinks it is a great game an' splashes The Twins. Though, there was that time that she let it go an' a sheep ate it. Ye could jist leave the leaves in the clean tea towel tae dry.

For picnic salads, keep lettuce in its ain box an' tear it into pieces when ye are ready tae use it. Tae another box, add onything ye fancy — e.g.: tomatoes, cucumber, potato, beetroot, cold boiled eggs, etc. — an' cover that in yer salad dressing if ye want. Lettuce leaves start tae wilt when bruised through tearing or when dressing is added tae them.

Beetroot Salad

Slice some pickled beetroot thinly. Mix with sliced boiled potato (cooled), chopped onion, chopped pickled gherkins, chopped cucumber, and low fat mayonnaise. Season with salt and pepper and a spoonful of cider vinegar.

Mix thoroughly and serve on lettuce leaves.

Things I tak' tae the But an' Ben, by Paw

Cairds	The Wine brewing book
Draughts	
Soor plooms	Auld claes for the berry pickin'
Fishing rod	
Scots Magazine	Sunday Post
Fishing flies	Book o' ghost stories

Bean Salad

A can of mixed pulses

3 tbsps finely chopped celery

2 tbsps red onions, chopped

1 tbsp cooked French beans

1 fresh tomato, chopped

1 clove garlic, crushed

Salt and black pepper to taste

2 tbsps mayonnaise

1 tsp tomato ketchup

2 tbsps balsamic vinegar.

Mix thoroughly and marinade for a few hours.

It's bean salad is it? I don't care whit it's been, whit is it noo?!

I've been waiting a' year to tell that joke!

26

An you should have waited bit longer Granpaw

Potato Salad

New tatties, wee waxy tatties boiled in their skins, are best for salad; they should be sliced about a quarter o' an inch thick.

Mix wi' finely chopped onion (one onion tae eight potatoes). Season weel an' mix three tablespoons cider vinegar an' three tablespoons mayonnaise together an' mix wi' potatoes.

Chives are nice instead o' onions. Ye could also add chopped mint or a few drops o' mint vinegar tae the dressing.

Chopped gherkins, capers and a guid splash o' cider vinegar and olive oil are braw and tasty wi' floury tatties.

Another guid dressing for tattie salad is made wi' a tub o' sour cream or créme fraiche, one tablespoon lemon juice, a bunch o' spring onions, chopped, one tablespoon olive oil, pepper an' salt.

Hame-Made Lemonade

Joe loves this in a flask wi' ice cubes on
ane o' his hikes if it's a warm day.

  6 large lemons
  5 oz granulated sugar
  2 ½ pints o' water

Wash the lemons thoroughly. Grate the
zest frae three o' the lemons. Dinna use
the white pith — it is bitter. Squeeze the
juice frae all the lemons an' add tae a
bowl wi' the grated zest. Add the sugar.
  Boil water an' pour into bowl. Cover
and leave overnight in a cool place. Next
day stir an' taste. Add more sugar if it
needs it. Strain through a sieve. Pour it
into bottles an' chill.
  For picnics put the chilled lemonade
into a flask wi' a little ice.

hame-made lemonade is boring
we like fizzy ginger

UCHENTOGLE
Open Sheep Dog Trials
ENTRY FORM

Owner: The Broon Twins

Dog: Horace

Age: Decrepit

Category: Big heeded swots

Experience: Kissed speccy Aggie McKechnie

Strengths: Reading and acting like a big Jessie

SCORE CHART

	POINTS LOST	POINTS WON
Outrun	by The Twins	
Lift	canny lift a pancake	
Fetch	us a fish slipper	
Shed	where Horace shood live	
Pen	where The Twins should live!	
TOTAL =	Just you two wait . . .	

Great Days at
The But an' Ben
A poem by Horace Broon

Locked up Glebe Street — caught the bu[s]
An awfy squeeze for all o' us.
   Off for great days at the But an' [Ben]
Berry-pickin', tatties tae,
Somethin' different every day.
   Happy times at the But an' Ben.
Singin' roon an open fire
Doonwind frae the fermer's byre.
   Cosy nights at the But an' Ben.
The Hielan' games was just the best.
I liked the caber tossin' test.
   Memories o' the But an' Ben.
Killiecrankie, castles, trips,
The seaside — sometimes fish an' chips.
   Days oot frae the But an' Ben.
Paw's ghost stories late at night
Sometimes gie an awfy fright.
   Family time at the But an' Ben.
Fishin' trips and climbin' tae,
We'll a' come back anither day.
   For great days at the But an' Ben.

Anither summer come an' gone
Anither pie, anither scone.
   Aye ... great days at the
   But an' Ben.

What I tak' tae the But an' Ben,
by Hen Broon

Walking boots and my
   guid socks
Maps, compass
Waterproof troosers
Cagoul
My guid hat

Plasters
Hip flask and a wee dram
The camping frying pan
Tent and camping stove
The Beano

What I take tae the But
an Ben, by Maggie

An Iron
Walking shoes
My new cagoul
My guid fluffy socks
My nice silky socks
Working clothes
Travel heated rollers
Waterproof make-up

These are all soups for taking in flasks — very smooth soups are best.

Aye, they leak better

Onion an' Watercress Soup

Very refreshing an' guid on a hot or cold day.

3 large onions
2 pints vegetable or chicken stock
1 cup single cream
2 tablespoons chopped watercress
2 ozs butter
Thick slice stale bread
A few bacon rinds

Peel an' slice the onions, cook them on a moderate heat in the butter till soft, but not coloured. This may tah' frae twenty tae thirty minutes.

Add the stock, the bacon rinds (tied in a bundle), an' the bread, cook gently for an hour, sieve an' reheat.

Jist afore ye dish it up remove the bacon rinds add the cream an' the watercress.

31

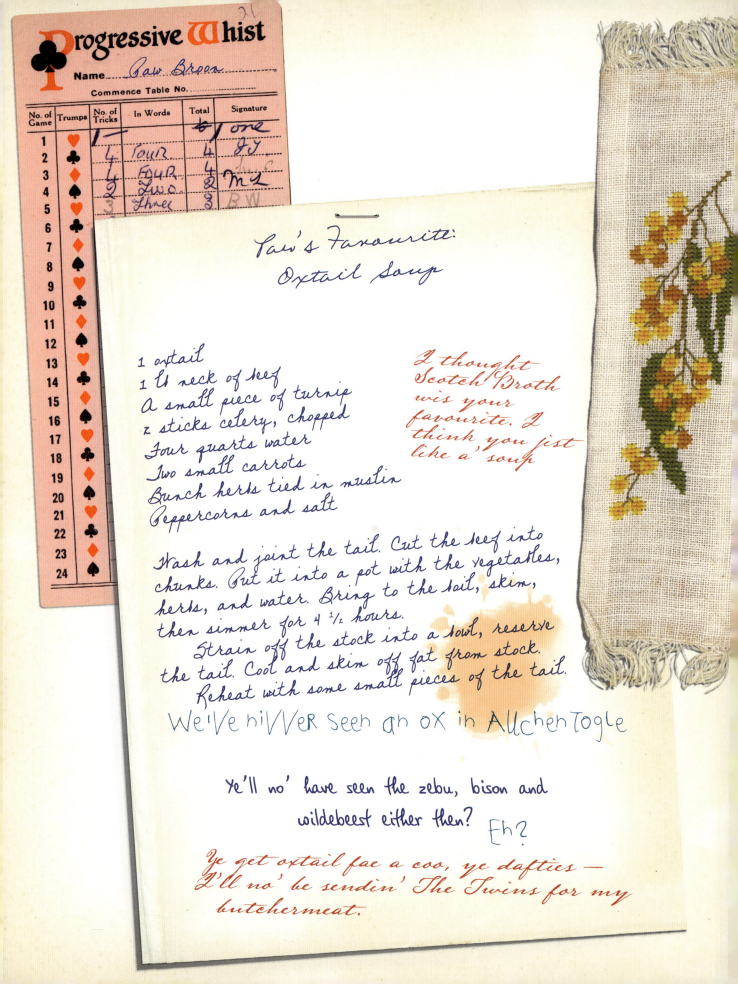

Paw's Favourite:
Oxtail Soup

1 oxtail
1 lb neck of beef
A small piece of turnip
2 sticks celery, chopped
Four quarts water
Two small carrots
Bunch herbs tied in muslin
Peppercorns and salt

I thought Scotch Broth wis your favourite. I think you jist like a' soup

Wash and joint the tail. Cut the beef into chunks. Put it into a pot with the vegetables, herbs, and water. Bring to the boil, skim, then simmer for 4 ½ hours.
Strain off the stock into a bowl, reserve the tail. Cool and skim off fat from stock. Reheat with some small pieces of the tail.

We'Ve hiVVer seen an ox in Auchentogle

Ye'll no' have seen the zebu, bison and wildebeest either then? Eh?

Ye get oxtail fae a coo, ye dafties — I'll no' be sendin' The Twins for my butchermeat.

Tomato Soup

2 sticks celery
1 wee onion
Butter
1 quart o' chopped fresh tomatoes
A teaspoonful sugar
1 pint chicken stock
Salt tae taste
Big handfu' o' fresh basil, chopped

Sweat the onion an' celery in a pot wi' a dod o' butter until soft. Then add the tomatoes, sugar an' stock into the pot, simmer for half an hour, stirring now an' then.

Strain tae get rid o' the tomato skins but leave some texture.

Fresh basil is lovely in this, add it at the end, a few minutes afore serving.

TWINS' TIP: YOU can Use a Tin
if YOU aRe in a hURRY

Barbecues

We canna hae barbecues at Glebe Street so we like tae hae plenty o' them at the But an' Ben. The only drawback is that you can bet that the smell o' Maw's hame-made sassidges cooking awa' will attract some bloomin' visitor or other!

Salmon Kebabs

2 salmon steaks
Marinade:
  Juice of half a lemon
  1/2 cup white wine
  1 tablespoon chopped fresh mint
  2 tablespoons chopped fresh parsley
  2 teaspoons chopped garlic
  1/4 cup olive oil
  Pinch salt

Tak oot Horace's minnows first

Put all marinade ingredients in an old jam jar with a well-fitting lid. Make sure the lid is on tight and shake vigorously. Cut the salmon into cubes and pour the marinade over. Marinate the salmon in the fridge for about half an hour. Put the salmon onto metal skewers. On the barbecue, cook on a moderate heat for about 5 minutes. Turn a few times to ensure even cooking.

Vegetable Skewers

2 courgettes, cut into thick slices
2 sweet peppers
2 red onions
1/2 pound whole fresh mushrooms
A small head of broccoli, broken up wee
Marinade: 1/3 cup vegetable oil
  1/2 cup balsamic vinegar
  2 tablespoons fresh thyme, chopped
  1 clove garlic, crushed
  1/2 teaspoon salt
  1/2 teaspoon black pepper
  1 tsp honey

Put marinade ingredients in a jam jar. Shake vigorously. Cut up vegetables into chunks all about the same thickness, put in a bowl, and pour marinade over. On metal skewers, thread vegetables together. On the barbecue, cook for about 15 minutes over a moderate heat. Turn regularly and baste with marinade.

Hame-Made Sassidges

I dinna bother putting them in skins—much too footery tae do at the But an' Ben.

4 ozs each o' pork, an' lean beef, minced
1 beaten egg
4 tablespoons white breadcrumbs
1 teaspoon salt
A guid pinch o' mixed herbs
A pinch grated nutmeg
A pinch white pepper
A wee drappie dripping

Mix these ingredients thoroughly tae a firm consistency. Shape into sausages, flour them, an' fry in the frying pan, wi a wee drappie dripping, till cooked through. Or put on the barbecue grill an' baste wi' oil.

Other barbie ideas:
chicken and beef and peppers on skewers
fresh fruit in a watermelon bowl
  (biodegradable bowl that can be
    discarded later!)
Bananas cooked in their skins (they
  come wi' their ain packaging)
pineapple and melon cubes on skewers
  and barbecued (honest, it's lovely)
fruit wrapped in foil (wi' spices)
tatties wrapped in foil (wi' seasoning)
pork and apple skewers

Onion Relish

3 large onions (red onions are nice for this)
2 teaspoons butter
1 teaspoon salt
$\frac{1}{2}$ teaspoon white pepper
A little sherry
$\frac{1}{4}$ teaspoon fresh ground pepper
$\frac{1}{3}$ cup tomato ketchup
$\frac{1}{3}$ cup dry white wine
1 teaspoon cider vinegar

Dice the onions (or cut in slices – whatever you prefer). Slowly fry the onions till soft but not brown, and add the salt, pepper and a small splash of sherry (1 or 2 tbsps). Cook till sherry has evaporated. Place in saucepan. Add the ketchup, white wine and cider vinegar, and slowly bring to the boil. Remove from the heat and taste. Pour into a sterilised glass jar and seal or eat straight away once cooled.

HOW TO COOK A HUSBAND!

The first thing to do is to catch him. Having done so, the method of cooking him to make a good dish must be studied. Many a good husband is spoiled in the cooking. Some women keep them constantly in hot water, while others freeze them with conjugal coldness; still others keep them in pickle all their lives. These women always serve them up with tongue sauce. Now it is not to be supposed that husbands will be tender and good if treated this way, but they are on the contrary very delicious when managed as follows:

Get a large jar called the jar of carefulness, which all good housewives have on hand. Place your husband in it and put him near the fire of conjugal love. Let the fire be fairly hot, especially let it be clear; above all let it be constant. Cover him over with affection, garnish him over with the spice of pleasantry, and if you add kisses and other confections let them be accompanied with a sufficient portion of secrecy, mixed with prudence and moderation.

Mrs. R. M. N. Johnson,
35 Idle Street.

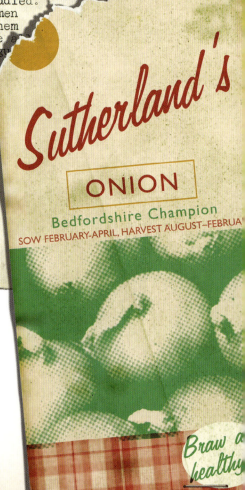

Sutherland's

ONION

Bedfordshire Champion

SOW FEBRUARY–APRIL, HARVEST AUGUST–FEBRUA

Braw a
healthy

Hame-Made Burgers

Burgers get a bad name — these yins are braw an' nothin' like yer fast food rubbish. This mak's aboot eight burgers.

2 lbs lean steak mince
2 slices bread made into breadcrumbs
1 egg, beaten
2 tablespoons tomato ketchup
Splash o' Worcesterhsire sauce
1 1/2 teaspoons salt
1/2 teaspoon cumin
1/2 teaspoon dry mustard
1/2 teaspoon fresh ground pepper
1/2 teaspoon white pepper
1 onion, chopped an' fried

In a large bowl, combine mince, breadcrumbs, beaten egg, ketchup, an' seasoning. Let the fried onion cool, then add to the mixture. Mix thoroughly. Shape into six patties. Fry for about 6 tae 10 minutes each side. Serve on a roll wi' onion relish. Recipe opposite.

Spit Roasting a Chicken at your Campfire

The Fire

Make the fire in a responsible way and make sure you are allowed to do so.

In the countryside, use an existing fire ring, if possible.

If not, then you could make what is called a mound fire. This enables you to build a fire on grass without scorching it. Lay a thick ground-cloth on the area. Place loose earth, sand or gravel on top to a thickness of about 5 inches. Make the mound much larger than the fire you are going to build.

Clear the surrounding area of dry leaves, sticks, etc., that might ignite and spread your fire (you can always use these as kindling anyway).

Never leave a fire unattended.

In your own garden you could make a pit. Lift a rectangular turf – making a shallow pit – so that you can replace the turf afterwards – and place rocks around the edges of the pit you've just made.

The fire must be well made and much larger than one you would make for a barbecue. Scrunch up paper and place on the bottom layer. Lay dry wood on top. Lay coals on top. Light paper and tend carefully till the coals turn white with red embers at the centre. Cooking times are long when cooking by spit roast, so you must be prepared to watch over your fire and your meat continuously. You will have to baste the meat and probably keep adding fuel to your fire but bear in mind that too much new fuel will cause the fire to smoke. To deliberately give your meat a smoked flavour you could add a small amount of wood.

Basting

Mix your baste, or marinade, up at home before you go camping and take it with you in a jar. Basting is essential for keeping the bird from drying out. A baste should contain an oil, an acid (like lemon juice or wine vinegar) and some salt. Use a brush (even an unused paintbrush will do). Of course, your baste can contain anything you please but these basic ingredients

will ensure a crispy skin without excessive burning. Watch out if your baste contains honey or sugar. These can be delicious but are perhaps best added in the last stages. Also take care if the baste contains pieces of garlic as burnt garlic can taste very unpleasant.

The Chicken

Smear bird with marinade. Push the spit up the rear of the chicken, through its body cavity, and out. Secure with clips. Use wire to tie the legs together around the spit and make sure the wings are tucked together too. Ensure that your fire is wide enough to cook the entire length of the bird.

Over the Fire

Position the spit roast on the rack and turn one complete revolution every one or two minutes. If you do not have a motorised spit this is going to have to be by hand.

The aim is to cook slowly but thoroughly, so be sure not to have the chicken too close to coals giving burned outer, and uncooked inner, flesh. Gradually turn the heat up. If you can hold your hand at the cooking level for at least 8, but no more than 12 seconds then this is probably a sufficient temperature.

Cooking Time

For a smallish chicken (around the 3lb mark) cook for around an hour. Test after 45 minutes by piercing the skin between the thigh and the body with a sharp knife. If juices run clear it is done – if there are specks of red blood it is certainly not.

Afterwards

Put the embers out with water, not soil. Lift up the ashes and scatter them around the area, thinly. Lift the groundsheet and replace the soil back where you found it. Replace the soil and turf if you dug a pit.

Maidie's Midge Repellent

don't do this at Glebe Street ha ha

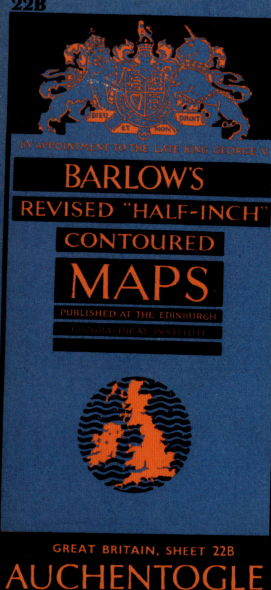

22B

BY APPOINTMENT TO THE LATE KING GEORGE V.

BARLOW'S REVISED "HALF-INCH" CONTOURED MAPS

PUBLISHED AT THE EDINBURGH GEOGRAPHICAL INSTITUTE

GREAT BRITAIN, SHEET 22B
AUCHENTOGLE

CLOTH 5/– NET

Spit-Roast Chicken

I sometimes completely cook the chicken in the oven and just finish it aff on the barbecue.

Ye need a quid fire going for this. It takes mair than an hour tae cook. We found an ancient spit roast in the big cupboard o' the But an' Ben. The last tenants must hae left it. It has a wee clockwork mechanism that ye wind up an' it will turn on its ain. Cook slowly, use the smallest chickens ye can get an' <u>never</u> <u>ever</u> eat chicken that is pink. After 1 hour, pierce wi' a knife. Only if the juices run clear is it cooked.

A 3lb chicken
Baste:
8 tbsps white wine
4 tbsps water
4 tbsps cooking oil

2 tsps black pepper
1 tsp salt
The juice o' 1 lemon
1 tbsp chopped, fresh rosemary

Mix up the baste above an' cover the bird. Continue tae baste the bird wi' this as it cooks, an' follow the instructions opposite that Hen got oot o' his Camping Around Scotland magazine.

41

Joe's Campfire Bread

We made this in army training. It might no' hae tasted like fine white bread but when ye were starvin' it was a rerr treat. Ye need tae tak' a big frying pan wi' ye. Heavy tae carry, but Hen an' I like a fry-up when we are camping so we are carrying it anyway. Ye can carry the dry ingredients all mixed up together in a bag or a tin ready tae add water an' a bit o' fat. If ye hae bacon (an' we usually dae!) ye can use the fat aff that when ye cook it, or ye could carry a wee bit o' hard vegetable fat or lard, wrapped in foil in a plastic box. Adding herbs makes this much nicer (I like a bit o' rosemary).

An' Rosemary speaks highly o' you too.

3 cups flour
2 cups milk powder
1 tsp baking powder
1 tsp sugar
1 cup water
Oil or fat for the pan

Add a cup o' water tae the dry ingredients. A plastic bag comes into its own here as a food mixer. Let's assume your frying pan is already greased an' hot frae fried bacon. Spread the thickish dough oot flat in the pan — quite thin. Turn after 7 tae 10 minutes. If it breaks dinna worry too much — we are not looking for prizes for presentation.

A Gardener's Year
One: Spring

Our quarterly step-by-step guide to maintaining your garden through the year. In this issue, spring is definitely in the air.

THE onset of spring varies across the country; even local variations can be marked. And it is not unusual for a warm spell to encourage new growth and spring blooms, only for sharp frosts to recur, killing buds and new sappy wood.

Spring is the busiest time for gardeners and lack of attention to beds and lawns at the beginning of the season will make it even more so.

In a good year, spring bulbs will be in flower from January to May, and planting summer bulbs, herbaceous plants and annuals in the spring will ensure a display of flowers lasting into the autumn.

There may be a lot of spring pruning to do. When inspecting frost-damaged plants, scratch the bark away to see if there is life underneath. If the damage is severe, cut back hard into healthy wood. Do not remove a plant until you are sure it is dead: the new season often brings surprises, even to experienced gardeners.

Bluebells are a welcome sight in spring.

EARLY SPRING

General Maintenance
—Complete digging and cultivation
—Mulch soil
—Tidy up paths and drives
—Weed borders
—Apply slug pellets (hidden under foliage)

Lawns
—Rake lawn vigorously
—Aerate with fork
—Fill hollows with sandy compost or adjust levels below turf
—Reseed worn areas
—Cut gently with blades set high
—Apply weedkiller
—Apply fertilizer

New Lawns
—Rake seedbed
—Feed soil with pre-seeding mixture
—Sow seed

Shrubs
—Prune buddleia, caryopteris, hardy fuchsia, hydrangea, ivies, spirea
—Plant rhododendrons and azaleas for spring display
—Continue planting
—Propagate by layering amelanchier, lilac, rhus, wintersweet
—Mulch and prune new shrubs

Flowers
—Plant herbaceous plants: acanthus, anemone, aster, campanula, delphinium, gaillardia, geranium, hollyhock, lupin, peony, phlox, potentilla, red hot poker, summer flowering bulbs (eg gladiolus, lily, acidanthera)
—Sow hardy annuals (eg cornflowers) outside, half-hardy annuals under glass, carnations and sweet peas
—Propagate by taking cuttings from dahlias and chrysanthemums
—Dead-head bulbs after flowering
—Remove dying leaves from bearded irises
—Lift and divide snowdrop bulbs

Roses
—Complete pruning of hybrid teas, floribundas and established miniature roses
—Plant new roses

Herbs
—Sow chervil, chives, dill, marjoram, parsley, sorrel

Vegetables
—Sow broad beans, celery, kohlrabi, parsnips, peas, broad beans, spinach. Carrots under glass in the south
—Plant early potatoes, asparagus, Jerusalem artichokes

Fruit
—Finish pruning
—Finish planting
—Mulch and feed young trees
—Plant strawberry runners
—Deal with pests (eg apple scab)

MID-SPRING

General Maintenance
—Mulch beds and borders
—Order seedlings (eg dahlias and tomatoes)
—Examine garden for bird damage and net if needed
—Hoe weeds

Lawns
—Mow frequently, lowering blades further for each cut
—Level humps and trim edges
—Apply weedkillers or grub out dandelions or plantains

New Lawns
—Cut the new grass gently to about 5 cm (2 in)

Shrubs
—Plant conifers and evergreen shrubs, pot-grown wall shrubs (eg clematis, honeysuckle, jasmine, vines, wisteria)
—Prune forsythias after flowering
—Cut back straggling branches on evergreens (eg magnolia, lavender)
—Stop side shoots on fuchsias
—Prune hard buddleia

Flowers
—Continue sowing hardy annuals (eg aster, sunflower, stock) outside, half-hardy annuals (eg alyssum, dahlia, phlox) under glass
—Plant out perennials (eg hollyhocks, peony, viola, bedding plants)
—Divide and replant established perennials if necessary
—Dead-head spring flowers (eg daffodils)

Roses
—Feed and hoe in fertilizer
—Apply mulch
—Apply weedkiller
—Begin spraying against black spot, mildew, etc
—Water newly planted roses if necessary

Vegetables
—Sow beetroot, broccoli, carrots (main crop), cauliflowers (late summer), onions, peas, winter cabbage
—Plant out late summer cabbages, onions raised under glass
—Finish planting late potatoes
—Remove rhubarb flowers

Fruit
—Protect bush fruit with nets against birds
—Continue to spray apples, blackcurrants, pears, strawberries and plums with pesticides—but not while blossoming
—Manure strawberries
—Spray peach flowers with water
—Secure trees and bushes

LATE SPRING

General Maintenance
—Keep slugs under control

Water frequently if necessary

Lawns
—Mow at least once a week with blades set low
—Continue to apply fertilizer
—Continue to apply weedkiller
—Apply fungicides if required

New Lawns
—Water frequently if necessary

Shrubs
—Continue planting
—Prune early-flowering trees and shrubs after flowering
—Mulch lilacs and remove suckers
—Water newly planted shrubs frequently if necessary

Flowers
—Sow biennials (eg Canterbury bell, forget-me-not, foxglove, polyanthus, poppy, sweet william, viola, wallflower)
—Plant out half-hardy annuals (eg dahlias)
—Plant lilies and asters
—Lift spring flowers, if necessary, to make room for bedding plants
—Weed alpine beds carefully
—Mulch sweet peas
—Hoe regularly round gladioli and sweet peas
—Dead-head spring flowers
—Support tall herbaceous plants

Roses
—Watch for pests and diseases (eg greenfly and black spot and spray at once if necessary)

Vegetables
—Erect canes to support runner beans
—Sow French beans and runner beans
—Plant Brussels sprouts
—Plant out spring cabbage
—Cover early potato shoots with earth to protect against frost

Fruit
—Water well and feed lightly if fruit is swelling
—Spray against pests, but not on open blossom
—Protect strawberries with straw
—Tie up new growth on blackberries
—Start thinning summer vines and thin out and mulch raspberries

---

SPRING DISPLAY
Flowers
Aubrieta, bergenia, bluebell, columbine, crocus, daffodil, fritillary, Lenten rose, narcissus, phlox, primrose, pyrethrum, mossy saxifrage (Peter Pan), scilla, spring gentian, tiarella, tulip, veronica

Trees And Shrubs
Azalea, buddleia, clematis (alpina), daphne, forsythia, Japanese flowering cherry, japonica, laburnum, lilac, magnolia, mahonia, ribes, rhododendron, viburnum, wisteria

Pick Yer Ain, Grow Yer Ain or Find it For Free

Berry picking, tattie howkin', foraging and gardening.

There's plenty to keep you amused while you look for the night's tea!

Horace's Tips For Finding Wild Food

Don't disturb wildlife.

Buy some books, take pictures and draw things. Get three souces of identification before you eat anything.

Find an expert to help you, if possible. Farmer Gray has helped me. Join a foraging group led by an expert.

Use your sense of smell, e.g., wild garlic plants have such a strong smell that, much like The Twins, you will smell them afore you see them.

Never, ever eat anything if you don't know what it is. Some plants are poisonous. Never eat a mushroom that you cannot 100% identify, they can be deadly!

Autumn is the best time for edible mushrooms.

Start with easy and obvious foods — wild strawberries, brambles and nettles are easy to spot.

Do not gather food from obviously contaminated ground (like the sites of old factories).

Don't pick fruit and plants that grow near busy roads.

Wash everything thoroughly. If you are eating berries as you pick them then don't gather from below waist-height (dogs ...). And look out for beasties!

If you are unsure ... DON'T EAT IT!

Wild things around the But an' Ben that can be eaten:

field mushrooms
brambles
elderberries
(-flowers)
gean berries
(wild cherries)
raspberries
wild rocket
dandelions
wild garlic
nettles

---

maggie dRinks neTTle Tea foR heR complekshUn. mebbe she shoULd wash heR face wi iT?

Mushroom Picking

- Ask for permission before you pick mushrooms on others' property or on nature reserves.
- Respect the environment.
- Only pick what you will use. Animals and insects will want to eat the mushrooms too.
- Do not pick mushrooms where the cap has not opened out.
- The mushrooms on the surface are only a tiny part of the entire fungus which lives under the ground. Do not damage this. Treat the surroundings with care and respect.
- Only pick what you can 100% identify. Some mushrooms are poisonous or even deadly and others are rare and should not be picked.

Wild Garlic

My favourite free food. Ye canna miss it aroond May time. Ye'll find it in the woods. It's easy tae recognise fae the braw flooers an' the even mair braw smell. Ye can use the leaves in salads an' sandwiches or pit them in the soup. The stems o' the flooers are sweet an' strong tastin', great snipped up in salads or on an omelette. The bulbs can be eaten tae, jist like normal garlic. Braw!

Wild Garlic

47

Mushroom Ketchup.

from Isa Brownlee

Mushrooms for this purpose must be picked when dry. Break them up into small pieces, place them in a stoneware pan and sprinkle with salt, allowing 1/4 lb of salt to each 3 1/2 lbs Mushrooms.

Let them stand for 3 days, frequently stirring and mashing them, to cause the juice to flow. Now strain and get all the juice possible by pressure.

To each quart of juice add :— 2 oz. of Salt, a few cloves, 1/4 oz of Peppercorns and 1/4 oz of whole ginger. If preferred, a pinch of cayenne and a little mace may be added. Boil slowly for 1 hour then strain. Bottle, cork well, and wax the corks over.

Some consider that more juice is obtained by heating the mushrooms in a jar in the oven.

NOTE. Double Ketchup is made by boiling ordinary ketchup down, a quart to a pint. There is no advantage in making this, except that smaller quantities can be used than the ordinary ketchup.

Potting Compost

3 parts garden
     soil
2 parts peat
(dug 1 year ago)
1 part garden
     sand

Sutherland's

CARROT

Autumn King

SOW MARCH–JULY, HARVEST AUGUST–DECEMBER

Braw an' healthy!

MR GILLESPIE'S Quality SEEDS

Garden Pea

Early Variety

Mushroom Paté

Granpaw kens whit mushrooms tae pick – they grow in Farmer McNab's field. If ye're no' sure whit yins tae pick, dinna pick them! Ye can get them at the farm shop ... though no' for free, admittedly.

2 tablespoons guid butter
1 large onion, chopped
1 ¼ lb flat, dark, field mushrooms
A pinch o' nutmeg
2 tablespoons parsley, chopped finely
A haundful o' wild garlic leaves, chopped finely
¼ teaspoon white pepper
¼ teaspoon salt
1 packet cream cheese

Slowly fry the onions, mushrooms, nutmeg in the butter till the onions are soft an' sweet. Mix in the other ingredients an' finish aff in a food mixer if you want a smooth paté.

Bramble Jeely

A' thae braw, free, wee brambles are jist too guid tae resist! Bramble jeely disna' keep awfy long so dinna mak' ower much. However, making jeely can be a richt footer so tae mak' it worth yer while mak' at least 2 lbs-worth. The jeely pan an' strainer are under the sink. There are aboot 20 jeely jaurs in the bottom o' the big press in the auld orange box.

Brambles, thoroughly washed
6 fl oz water for every 1lb of fruit
The juice o' 1 lemon for every 1lb fruit
1lb sugar for every pint of juice

Simmer the berries in water for 15 minutes. When completely soft add the lemon juice and strain through a sterlised muslin or a jelly bag overnight. Measure the juice. For every pint add 1lb sugar. Dissolve the sugar ower a low heat, then let it boil. Test after 10 minutes on a cold plate. Push the syrup wi' your finger an' if it wrinkles it has set, if not, keep boiling. Pour intae sterilised jars an' top wi' waxed paper.

A Gardener's Year
Two: Summer

Our quarterly step-by-step guide to maintaining your garden through the year. In this issue we show you how to prepare your garden during the summer months.

WITH the bustle of spring receding and the garden filling with colour, the gardener can relax and enjoy the warm summer days. But there is still plenty to do to keep everything looking its best. Borders and lawns must be thoroughly watered, hedges trimmed and blooms dead-headed— a few yellow leaves in a formal area can spoil the whole effect.

When going away on holiday have somebody check on the garden. Drought is the worst enemy. Mulching helps matters, but thorough watering is essential to promote growth, even if there are summer rains.

This is not the usual time to plant but it can be done (particularly if the plants are container grown), provided the roots are thoroughly soaked beforehand and extra attention is paid to the plants' subsequent welfare.

Early summer will herald the blossoming of the clematis.

EARLY SUMMER

General Maintenance
—Weed, hoe and water as necessary
—Spray against pests and diseases

Lawns
—Mow once a week in different directions, setting the blades low. If the weather is very hot and dry, leave a fine mulch of clippings on the lawn
—Apply weedkillers and feed

Shrubs
—Dead-head and prune shoots that have just flowered on shrubs (eg deutzia, lilac, philadelphus) to encourage new growth next year
—Dead-head laburnum flowers (poisonous), rhododendrons
—Trim broom with sharp shears to prevent seeding
—Plant out fuchsias
—Propagate by layering young shoots of clematis
—Take cuttings of softwood shoots of cotoneaster, deutzia, fuchsia, hypericum

Flowers
—Complete planting out half-hardy annuals grown from seed (eg dahlias)
—Set out biennial seedlings in rows
—Support tall annuals with canes
—Dead-head late spring/early summer flowers (eg delphiniums, lupins, violas) to encourage a late crop of flowers
—Cut back early-flowering herbaceous plants to just above the ground
—Lift tulips and other spring-flowering bulbs that need to be divided and replanted when leaves turn yellow
—Pinch out main stems of dahlias and chrysanthemums to promote bushy growth
—Take cuttings of pinks
—Water copiously (in the evenings if possible) despite summer rains, especially new and transplanted plants.

Roses
—Spray with systemic insecticide to prevent aphids, and spray against black spot and mildew
—Hoe around the bases

Vegetables
—Plant broccoli, Brussels sprouts, cauliflowers, marrows, savoy cabbages, winter cabbages, leeks, outdoor tomatoes
—Stake and pinch out runner beans and tomatoes
—Earth up late potatoes

Fruit
—Maintain spraying programme against pests
—Check for slug damage. Lay pellets if necessary
—Harvest strawberry crop
—Train fruit trees if necessary
—Prune gooseberries

MIDSUMMER

General Maintenance
—Continue to weed, hoe and water
—Continue to spray against pests and diseases
—Dead-head and cut flowers

Lawns
—Continue to water well
—Mow regularly
—Clip edges with shears
—Apply weedkiller and fertilizer as necessary

Shrubs
—Continue to dead-head deciduous shrubs
—Clip hedges
—Propagate by layering passion flower, wisteria and shrub roses

Flowers
—Continue to dead-head flowers to encourage further flowering
—Support tall plants
—Water well, especially sweet peas and gladioli
—Continue to lift spring-flowering bulbs that need to be stored and replanted
—Plant out perennials (eg wallflowers)

Roses
—Continue to spray against pests
—Cut blooms for decoration and dead-head the rest
—Hoe fertilizer into the soil

Vegetables
—Sow beet and lettuce
—Continue to plant broccoli, Brussels sprouts, kale, leeks, cabbage
—Start to lift and store onions and shallots as tops turn yellow
—Water shallow-rooted crops in dry weather

Fruit
—Harvest soft fruit
—Prune currants and raspberries after fruiting
—Summer-prune apples and pears where appropriate
—Train branches as desired
—Spray against pests
—Weed thoroughly around trees and bushes
—Support heavily fruiting plum branches
—Tidy up strawberry beds
—Protect against birds with netting if necessary

LATE SUMMER

General Maintenance
—Continue weeding, hoeing and watering
—Continue to spray against pests and diseases
—Continue to dead-head and cut flowers
—While on holiday, ask neighbours to pick sweet peas and vegetables, and water occasionally

Lawns
—Mow and water regularly
—Continue to trim lawn edges
—Continue applying weedkillers as necessary

New Lawns
—Dig over and apply fertilizer to sites for new lawns
—Sow lawn seed a week later

Shrubs
—Continue to prune shrubs (eg wisteria, rambler roses) after flowering
—Take half-ripe cuttings of garrya, hydrangea and wisteria for pot culture in cold frame
—Propagate by layering rhododendrons

Flowers
—Continue dead-heading
—Cut blooms on gladioli and sweet peas
—Disbud chrysanthemums, leaving one flower per stem, to make large blooms
—Order spring-flowering bulbs for autumn planting
—Plant out well-grown perennial seedlings

Roses
—Continue to cut blooms and dead-head
—Continue to spray against pests
—Do not fertilize since this encourages late growth

Vegetables
—Sow hardy onions, spinach, spring cabbage, winter lettuce
—Plant winter greens
—Earth up leeks, kale and potatoes
—Crop regularly and dig and fertilize the ground after cropping

Fruit
—Continue summer pruning of apples and pears where appropriate
—Prune shoots that have borne fruit on peaches, nectarines, cherries, blackberries, loganberries and hybrid berries
—Plant strawberries and rooted strawberry runners
—Support heavily laden plum branches
—Crop regularly

SUMMER DISPLAY

Flowers
African lily, begonia, carnation, chrysanthemum, cornflower, delphinium, gazania, hollyhock, iris, lady's mantle, lupin, peony, phlox, pink, poppy, primula, pyrethrum, rose, snapdragon, stock, sweet pea, verbena, veronica

Trees and Shrubs
Buddleia, catalpa, cistus, clematis, deutzia, fuchsia, honeysuckle, hydrangea, laburnum, lavendar, olearia, passion flower, potentilla, willow-leaved pear

Quick Pea an' Mint Soup

Granpaw usually has a few rows o' pea pods in his gairden at hame, an' sometimes if he has too many plants he grows some up the back wall o' the But an' Ben. If I get the chance I'll pick them for dinner — usually the bairns have eaten them a'! Ye can aye use frozen peas.

We PUT e peas OOR Pea OOTERS

4 onions, chopped
2 oz butter
1 1/2 lbs fresh peas
1 3/4 pints chicken stock
Salt an' pepper
4 tbsp chopped fresh mint leaves

GRanpaw says we're twa peas in a pod

Sweat the chopped onions in the butter until soft an' sweet. Add the peas an' boiling chicken stock an' simmer for 5 minutes. Pass through a sieve or liquidise. Add salt an' pepper an' mint an' taste it.

Add a dollop o' double cream if ye fancy. Enough for aboot eight folk.

Cauliflower Soup

2 ozs of butter
2 onions, chopped
Two pints chicken stock
1 small head cauliflower, chopped small
One or two tablespoonfuls chopped
  watercress
One cup single cream

Melt the butter in a pan. Add the onions cut into rings, cover tightly, and leave them to cook over a low heat for 20 minutes.

Add the cauliflower and stock and bring to the boil and cook for another 40 minutes. Pass through a sieve and stir in the watercress and cream. Simmer for a few minutes and serve.

Chilli Vinegar

Cut 20 small, very hot red chillies in two, put them in a jar, and cover with a pint of vinegar, infuse for a fortnight, then strain.

You can use these chillies again but this time infuse in vinegar for a fortnight but with only half a pint of vinegar.

Raspberry Vinegar
From Eileen Smith

To every 4lbs rasps, add 1 pint vinegar. Crush rasps before adding vinegar. Leave to stand for approx 3 days. Squeeze through muslin (doubled). Add 3/4 lb sugar per 1 pint juice.
Bring to boil, just (otherwise it thickens if boiled too long).
Bottle when cold.

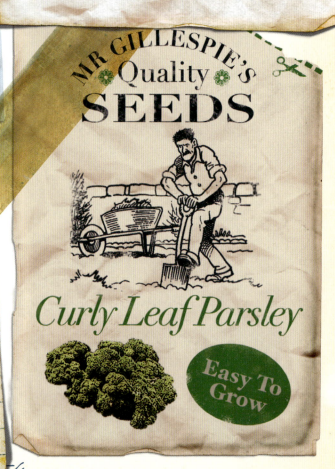

MR GILLESPIE'S
Quality
SEEDS

Curly Leaf Parsley

Easy To Grow

Nettle Soup

Nettles mak' lovely soup. Wear gloves tae pick them an' only pick the youngest tips. Ye'll need a whole load o' nettles because they cook awa tae nothing. It's a nice refreshing summer soup.

1 sweet onion, chopped
1 tablespoon salted butter
A whole potful o' nettles
1 1/2 pints chicken stock
A peeled, grated tattie
White pepper
Black pepper
A glug o' cream

Cook the onion till soft. Wash the nettles (still use your rubber gloves!). Then blanch them wi' boiling water (this means scald them wi' a wee drappie boiling water). This will shrink them doon. Drain. Add tae the onions an' then add the stock, potato an' seasoning. Simmer for under an hour an' then pass through a sieve. Afore ye dish it up add cream an' more seasoning if needed. Serve hot, or chilled if ye're posh.

BERRY PICKING
at
Gowkthrapple Farm

3d a pound

* Children with berry-stained faces will be x-rayed.

BEETROOT

- Cook it in boiling salted water; the time depends very much on the age and size of the root, but when ready it feels rather like rubber. Strain, and when cool, rub off the skin.
- It may also be put into a jar with a few peppercorns and enough boiling vinegar to cover it, and used, when cold, as a salad.
- The tips of the beetroot, if young, may be cooked like young cabbage.

This is the best beetroot chutney. I've written it oot in the Prize Cooking section, page 121

Sutherland's
BEETROOT
Bolthardy
SOW MARCH-JULY, HARVEST AUGUST–DECEMBER

Braw an healthy!

Beetroot Chutney

3 lb Beetroot Boil and skin
1 lb Onions   1 lb baking apples
1 Pint Vinegar ½ lb Sugar
1 Teaspoon Salt
1 - - Ground Ginger

Chop Apples & Onions in pan with Vinegar Simmer till tender Add sugar, Chopped Beetroot, Salt & ~~Spice~~ Ginger Simmer for 20 minutes and Bottle.
Rub bottom of pan with a little butter keeps if from sticking

58

Nettle Soup

Nettles mak' lovely soup. Wear gloves tae pick them an' only pick the youngest tips. Ye'll need a whole load o' nettles because they cook awa tae nothing. It's a nice refreshing summer soup.

1 sweet onion, chopped
1 tablespoon salted butter
A whole potful o' nettles
1 ½ pints chicken stock
A peeled, grated tattie
White pepper
Black pepper
A glug o' cream

Cook the onion till soft. Wash the nettles (still use your rubber gloves!). Then blanch them wi' boiling water (this means scald them wi' a wee drappie boiling water). This will shrink them doon. Drain. Add tae the onions an' then add the stock, potato an' seasoning. Simmer for under an hour an' then pass through a sieve. Afore ye dish it up add cream an' more seasoning if needed. Serve hot, or chilled if ye're posh.

A Gardener's Year
Three: Autumn

Our quarterly step-by-step guide to maintaining your garden through the year. In this issue we show you how to prepare your garden for Autumn.

AS the days begin to shorten and temperatures drop, the pace of activity in the garden increases once more. Autumn is the beginning of the gardening year.

Now is the time to begin planting shrubs, herbaceous plants and bulbs. For roots to become quickly established, the soil must be warm and moist; as soon as these conditions prevail, use them.

The garden in summer is usually a place of high colour. Autumnal hues, though more muted, can be equally breathtaking. Look around and see if the display in your garden has this seasonal continuity.

Indian summers will prolong the growth of grass and weeds despite the leaves falling from the trees. Carry on with regular routine maintenance for as long as it is required; in milder areas, the grass may still need mowing as December approaches.

There is a lot of pruning to be done, and gardens surrounded by deciduous trees will be assailed by leaves. If you burn the leaves, remember the soil will need replenishing as the natural cycle has been broken. Install compost bins if you can, and keep bonfire ash to spread as potash.

By the time Christmas arrives, the garden should have been put to bed for the winter—neat and tidy with tender plants protected against sharp frosts and cold, dry winds.

Foliage is a rich source of garden colour in autumn.

EARLY AUTUMN

General Maintenance
—Continue weeding
—Tidy up leaves as they begin to fall

Lawns
—Mow until end of growing season when grass is dry
—Aerate by spiking and top-dress with sharp sand if soil is heavy
—Re-seed worn patches

New Lawns
—Prepare to make new lawns from turf (and seed in milder areas)

Shrubs
—Main planting season begins
—Take cuttings of hardy shrubs
—Remove dead wood and prune summer-flowering shrubs
—Water newly planted shrubs
—Secure plants against wind damage

Flowers
—Plant spring-flowering bulbs (eg daffodils, narcissi) in succession
—Plant indoor bulbs (eg hyacinths) in pots
—Transplant perennials and biennials sown earlier (eg wallflowers)
—Check layering of pinks
—Divide layers that would have rooted and plant under frames
—Sow hardy annuals
—Cut down perennials after flowering

Roses
—Continue to dead-head
—Spray regularly against pests
—Prune climbers and ramblers

Vegetables
—Harvest root vegetables
—Plant winter crops (eg winter lettuce, spring cabbage) under cloches
—Sow carrots under cloches

Fruit
—Harvest blackberries as they ripen, then prune and train young growth.
—Pick peaches, nectarines, plums and damsons, then prune

—Complete summer pruning of apples and pears
—Check ties and supports
—Plan for new planting later in the season

MID-AUTUMN

General Maintenance
—Cover ponds with netting to catch leaves
—Sweep up fallen leaves and save for compost

Lawns
—Aerate and scarify
—Lay new turves if desired

Shrubs
—Plant trees, shrubs and climbers in well-prepared ground
—Take hardwood cuttings
—Propagate by layering daphne, fothergilla, witch hazel, etc

Flowers
—Plant autumn-flowering to early spring-flowering herbaceous plants (eg Christmas rose, golden rod, pinks, polyanthus, rudbeckia, viola, wallflower)
—Continue planting bulbs (eg anemone, bluebell, chionodoxa, crocus, cyclamen, daffodil, fritillary, hyacinth, montbretia, narcissus, nerine, schizostylis, scilla, tulip)
—Sow alpines in a cold frame
—Complete sowing hardy annuals
—Plant out carnations layered earlier
—Divide and replant overcrowded perennials after flowering
—Move indoor-germinated sweet peas out under a cold frame
—Lift and store gladioli, dahlia corms and tubers

Roses
—Prepare new beds for planting
—Take cuttings of floribundas and ramblers

Vegetables
—Continue to plant winter crops (spring cabbage, winter lettuce, etc) under cloches
—Watch out for slug damage to winter vegetables and hoe around them regularly
—Earth up leeks and celery

Fruit
—Begin planting fruit trees and bushes
—Prune branches that have fruited on gooseberries, raspberries and canes
—Root prune plums and damsons
—Continue to pick apples and pears
—Spray peaches against leaf curl

LATE AUTUMN

General Maintenance
—Complete autumn digging
—Condition the soil if necessary

Lawns
—Rake off leaves
—Aerate
—Complete turving

Shrubs
—Continue to plant trees and shrubs if weather remains mild; protect less robust species with windbreaks
—Complete hardwood cuttings of aucuba, holly, ivy, laurel, poplar, etc, and put in a cold frame

Flowers
—Complete planting perennials
—Continue tidying and cutting back herbaceous flowers
—Remove bedding plants as they fade
—Store (in frost-free place or take indoors or into greenhouse) woodier plants (eg fuchsias, geraniums)
—Plant in prepared beds
—Prune climbing roses
—Complete cuttings

Vegetables
—Pick Brusselsprouts and leeks
—Sow broad beans for an early crop
—Cultivate soil after cropping

Fruit
—Plant all fruit trees and bushes (eg apple, blackberry, blackcurrant, cherry, damson, gooseberry, loganberry, nectarine, peach, pear, plum, raspberry, redcurrant, strawberry, vine)
—Prune apples, pears, blackberries, loganberries and fruit trees
—Mulch young trees

AUTUMN DISPLAY

Flowers
Anemone (*japonica*), chrysanthemum, cyclamen (*alpinum*), gaillardia (*Helenim autumnale*), kaffir lily, nasturtium, nerine, rose, rudbeckia, statice (*Limonium latifolium*)

Trees and Shrubs
Amelanchier, azalea (for foliage), barberry, callicarpa, cotinus, cotoneaster, firethorn, fuchsia, hawthorn, hebe, mahonia, maple, rowan, euonymus, sumach, viburnum

How Tae Dry Mushrooms

At some times o' the year there are that many mushrooms ye canna eat them a'! So it is a guid idea tae dry some for the winter.

Pick nice anes - because flavour is lost in the drying process an' ye need tae start aff wi' really guid anes.

Choose large, open mushrooms, wipe clean, tak' oot the stalks. Spead them oot on a tray, so the air can get roon them. Mak' sure they dinna touch.

Dinna throw awa' the stalks. Ye can mak' a guid stock oot o' them if ye boil in salted water.

Dry in a 140°F oven (60°C) for 3 or 4 hours.

Or, tae save money if a lot o' cooking is being done on the stove (an' that area is quite warm) thread the mushroom tops on thin twine an' hang them near the stove until they have completely dried. This may tak' a day or twa. When dry, store in paper bags.

Soak the dried m,ushrooms afore use. Best in stews as the texture is toughened by drying.

BERRY PICKING
at
Gowkthrapple Farm

3d a pound

• *Children with berry-stained faces will be x-rayed.*

BEETROOT

- Cook it in boiling salted water; the time depends very much on the age and size of the root, but when ready it feels rather like rubber. Strain, and when cool, rub off the skin.
- It may also be put into a jar with a few peppercorns and enough boiling vinegar to cover it, and used, when cold, as a salad.
- The tips of the beetroot, if young, may be cooked like young cabbage.

This is the best beetroot chutney. I've written it oot in the Prize Cooking section, page 121

page 121

Sutherland's BEETROOT

Bolthardy

SOW MARCH–JULY, HARVEST AUGUST–DECEMBER

Braw an healthy!

Beetroot Chutney

3 lb Beetroot Boil and skin
1 lb Onions   1 lb cooking apples
1 Pint Vinegar ½ lb Sugar
1 Teaspoon Salt
1 — — Ground Ginger

Chop Apples & Onions in pan with Vinegar Simmer till tender Add sugar, chopped Beetroot, Salt & ~~Spice~~ Ginger Simmer for 20 minutes and Bottle.
Rub bottom of pan with a little butter keeps it from sticking

58

Aipple Chutney

2 1/2 lbs peeled, cored apples
1 1/2 lbs soft brown sugar
1 1/2 ozs garlic
2 teaspoons ground ginger
2 teaspoons peppercorns
2 teaspoons coriander seeds
8 ozs onions
1 lb seeded raisins or sultanas
4 teaspoons salt
1 pint brown vinegar

Chop the aipples, raisins, onions, an' garlic.

Tie the peppercorns an' coriander seeds in a muslin bag (mind an' tah' them oot afore ye pot it). Add the sugar. Mix it a' weel, put into a pot, add the vinegar, an' cook for an hour, or longer, if the aipples still seem hard. Stir frequently.

This should make aboot 5 lbs o' chutney.

Fill dry, hot jars and screw on lids, or use cellophane jam covers. Seal jars well and store in a cool cupboard.

 sterilise jars:
ash thoroughly in hot soapy water. Rinse thoroughly.
ace in a cool oven for 10 minutes.   59

Carrot Fritters

Carrot fritters are absolutely delicious. Cut into circles diagonally, if ye ken whit I mean. Deep fry till golden and serve wi' wild leaf salad and shredded pickled beetroot ... to make it healthy, ha ha.

3 large carrots, cut in circles
The batter:
   5 oz self-raising flour
   About 2 tbsps malt vinegar
   8 fl oz beer (or fizzy water)
   Guid pinch salt
A deep pan of oil or hard
   vegetable fat

Mix the batter ingredients together to make the consistency of thick cream. Heat the fat till you see a haze above it. Test the fat with a dribble of batter. If it quickly bubbles and browns the fat is hot enough. Dip the raw carrot in the batter and carefully drop in the hot oil.

Paw's Dandelionade

I made this as a boy wi' flowers fae the local park.

A bag o' open dandelion flowers
1 lb sugar
The juice an' peel o' an orange
The juice an' peel o' a lemon
Enough water tae almost fill yer pot

Put dandelion flowers an' sugar in the pot. Add water and simmer for aboot 30 minutes. Squeeze the orange an' lemon an' add the juice tae the pot. Add the peel tae.
   Simmer 10 mins mair. Strain and cool. Drink with ice in it.
   Using this recipe as a guide, ye could also make drinks oot o' ither edible leaves and fruits such as nettles elderberries and elderflowers.
   [For Mint-ade use a bag of mint leaves instead of dandelion, leave oot the lemon an' orange, an' add a grated apple and apple juice instead.]

Carrots help you see in the dark

dandelions make you pee in the dark

Twins!!

Dandelion Tea

Infuse one ounce of dandelion in a jug with a pint of boiling water for fifteen minutes; sweeten with brown sugar or honey, and drink several tea-cupfuls during the day. The use of this tea is recommended as a safe remedy in all bilious affections; it is also an excellent beverage for persons afflicted with dropsy.

Carrot an' Coriander Soup

2 onions, chopped
1 clove wild garlic, finely chopped (or
    use leaves or stems, finely chopped)
1 oz butter
2 teaspoons ground coriander
2 pints chicken stock
1 lb carrots, peeled an' grated
Fresh coriander, chopped
Salt an' white pepper tae taste

Sweat the onions an' garlic in the pot
wi' butter an' the ground coriander. Add
the chicken stock an' grated carrots,
bring tae the boil, an' then simmer for
about half an hour. Pass through a
sieve or liquidise. Stir in the chopped
coriander, add salt an' pepper tae taste,
an' dish up wi' a wee drappie cream in
the centre if ye fancy.

Conkers—The Rules

Gather the conkers fae the ground — there's nae need to go flinging things intae trees tae get them.

There are twa players, each wi' a conker on a string (or a shoelace... easier tae thread through).

Each taks it in turns tae hit the other person's conker wi' theirs.

The conker being hit must be held still — moving is cheating!

If it is moving your opponent has the right tae straighten it and tak' another turn.

Haud it tight, 'cause if ye drap it, ye should be prepared for "playground rules" to tak ower and for spectators tae try an' stamp on it!

The winner is the player left wi' an intact conker, while his or her opponent's conker is broken.

Dinna be a jessie — be prepared tae get yer knuckles hit accidentally, it might sting but it'll no kill ye! However, dinna be a gonk an' get too near anybody's face.

Scoring

A winning conker's score depends on how many it has smashed. A conker that has broken one is a ones-er, etc. Also, Horace says: "a winning conker takes on the ghosts o' vanquished conkers!" The score o' a broken conker is added tae a winning conker's score plus one. E.g. a fives-er that smashes another fives-er becomes an elevenser-er, etc.

The sweet chestnut is said to have been introduced to Britain by the Romans.

They ground them up tae mak' 'chestnut porridge'. You canna eat horse chestnuts, they are very bitter and contain a chemical toxic to humans.

Paw's porridge is toxic to humans

To make champion conkers soak them in vinegir and then dry oot in a hot oven

No, no, no! Dinna soak in vinegar and dry them oot, that makes them too brittle. Jist pit all your conkers in a slow oven (120°C, 250°F, gas mark 1) for aboot twa hours.

When they are cool enough, pierce a hole wi' a darning needle and thread a foot-long piece of string.

Naw! — the best way is tae use a conker that is years old. Pierce it wi' a skewer, thread it an' then put it awa' till the next season at least. I've got conkers that are 50 years auld!

There's nae answer tae that.

Sweet-Chestnut Burgers

Ye canna eat horse chestnuts, mind — they are only guid for conkers. It's sweet chestnuts that can be eaten — if ye dinna ken the difference then dinna eat them! They are no' native trees but there are some in the woods near Glair Castle that Mr Willison's grandfaither planted years ago. He'll let ye gather some.

2 ozs butter
¼ pint tomato pulp (or passata)
2 weel-beaten eggs
1 wee onion, chopped
2 ozs chopped sweet chestnuts
1 oz breadcrumbs (or more for binding)
Pepper an' salt

Fry the onion in the butter till soft, add the tomato, an' nuts an' stir till the mixture just boils. Put in a bowl an' cool, then add some breadcrumbs, one beaten egg an' seasoning an' bind together in burger shapes. Dip in the ither beaten egg an' roll in breadcrumbs. Slowly fry in oil till raw eggs are cooked an' breadcrumbs are a braw broon colour.

A Gardener's Year
Four: Winter

Our quarterly step-by-step guide to maintaining your garden through the year. Here we take you through the preparations a gardener needs to make during the winter months.

THOUGH the garden can retain interest throughout the year, the winter months do involve less work for the gardener. Now is the time to have mowers serviced, order seeds, mend fences and repoint walls.

There are usually plenty of bright, sunlit days, however cold they may be, and light is at its clearest. Deciduous trees, bare of leaves, show structure. This is the best time to prune them, before the sap begins to rise.

Continue checking plants against weather damage. Planting may continue when the ground is neither frozen nor water-logged but, ideally, autumn and spring are better times.

Take care not to walk on the soil after heavy rains as the resulting compaction will then have to be corrected. Heavier soils will benefit greatly from being cultivated so that the frosts can break down lumps on the surface. Whatever the type of soil, cultivation in winter is desirable to improve aeration and to expose pests to the birds; robins are not being especially friendly when they see a fork in action—they just know a good thing when they see it.

It is evergreen trees and shrubs that give the best display of colour in winter.

WINTER DISPLAY
Flowers
Christmas rose, crocus, hyacinth, Lenten rose, snowdrop, stylosa, iris, winter aconite

Trees and Shrubs
Aucuba (*japonica*), Chinese juniper, cypress, daphne (*mezereum*), false cypress, flowering cherry (*Prunus subhirtella*), garrya (*elliptica*), heather, honeysuckle (*Lonicera fragrantissima*), mahonia, pine (*sylvestris*), pyracantha, skimmia (*japonica*), strawberry tree, winter jasmine, witch hazel (*Hamamelis mollis*)

EARLY WINTER
General Maintenance
—Fork over beds when frost-free
—Tidy garden, including sweeping up leaves
—Protect stand-pipes and taps against frost
Lawns
—Check for badly drained areas and remedy
—Prepare areas to be sown in spring
—Service lawn mower
Shrubs
—Continue planting when ground is frost-free and not waterlogged
—Prune shrubs after flowering for bushy summer foliage, particularly elder and sorbaria
—Ensure shrubs are secured against strong winds
—Mulch azaleas, rhododendrons, camellias, etc
Flowers
—Hoe tulip beds and spray with insecticide
—Protect tender plants such as sweet peas against rapid thawing after frosts by covering frames with matting
—Check bulbs and corms in store
Roses
—Prune lightly to prevent wind rock
—Continue planting when ground is not waterlogged or frost-bound
Vegetables
—Check vegetables in store and discard anything rotten
—Dig over sites for next season's runner beans
—Order seeds
Fruit
—Check stored fruit and for wind damage to ties and stakes
—Prune vines, fruit bushes and trees when weather is mild
—Complete root pruning
—Grease-band and tar-wash fruit trees to protect against infestation

MIDWINTER
General Maintenance
—Continue planting and ordering seedlings
—Check garden structures
Lawns
—Continue aerating
—Rake out moss and remove dead leaves
Shrubs
—Mulch azaleas, rhododendrons, camellias, etc, if not already done
—Ensure young shrubs are protected against frost
—Brush heavy snow off branches to prevent them snapping under the weight
Flowers
—Plant lilies, antirrhinums, etc, provided soil is not waterlogged or frost-bound
—Divide perennials
—Check chrysanthemums for waterlogging and aerate with a fork if necessary; check for grey mould and spray with fungicide
—Complete dead-heading
—Bring bulbs indoors (eg hyacinths) for flowering
Roses
—Continue planting if weather permits
Vegetables
—Order seeds
—Apply lime when digging
—Sow (in mild areas) early vegetables (eg broad beans, peas)
—Plant rhubarb; cover with straw and manure
—Check stored vegetables and discard anything rotten
Fruit
—Continue spraying and tar-washing
—Continue pruning
—Continue to check ties and stakes
—Check stored fruit and discard anything rotten

LATE WINTER
General Maintenance
—Service gardening equipment
Lawns
—Brush with a birch broom on dry days to remove worm-casts
—Continue aerating
—Dress with fine sand
—Repair edges
—Continue preparing for spring seeding by raking soil to fine tilth
Shrubs
—Begin planting in mild weather
—Prune hard summer-flowering clematis
Flowers
—Plant (in mild weather) anemones, lilies, buttercups, primroses
—Sow hardy annuals under glass till late in season if weather is mild
—Divide large clumps of perennials
—Sprinkle rock garden with slug pellets
—Prepare ground for sweet peas
—Dig beds for annuals and biennials
Roses
—Continue planting if weather permits
Vegetables
—Sow early peas and beans when weather is mild; put carrots and parsnips under cold frame
—Plant shallots in shallow drills
Fruit
—Continue pruning except during frosts
—Continue grease-banding and tar-washing

A Poke An' A Stalk

A treat for the bairns. This is a wee bit like a cheap sherbet dip. Rhubarb is hinna like a soor lollipop that has its ain stick.

Paw says: Clean yer teeth after eating this.

Granpaw says: Ye only need tae clean the teeth ye want tae keep!

You will need:

A broon paper bag
Sugar
A young, thin rhubarb stalk (mind the leaves are poisonous)

Cut the corner aff the paper poke. Fill the corner wi' sugar. Cut the rhubarb stalk into 6-inch sticks. Gie to your bairns. Stand back and enjoy watching their expressions change when they taste the sweet sugar and then the soor rhubarb. Innocent pleasures!

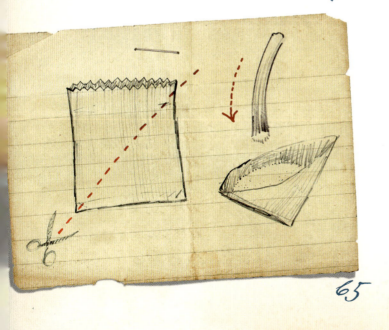

mock duck and the sauce made from a syrup of wild cherries—also known as gean berries—with the roast is quite a delicious contrast to the meat.

For your amusement, I include an extract from Francatelli's respected tome, *A Plain Cookery Book for the Working Classes*, with his very indiosyncratic advice for catching your own food.

Nowadays we would never dream of catching small wild birds. In addition to the fact that many are considered endangered, it seems frankly barbarous to encourage one's offspring to be setting traps in one's garden for supper. Times are hard but we can be inventive in other ways to make our rations go further.

No. 24. A PUDDING MADE OF SMALL BIRDS.

Industrious and intelligent boys who live in the country, are mostly well up in the cunning art of catching small birds at odd times during the winter months. So, my young friends, when you have been so fortunate as to succeed in making a good catch of a couple of dozen of birds, you must first pluck them free from feathers, cut off their heads and claws, and pick out their gizzards from their sides with the point of a small knife, and then hand the birds over to your mother, who, by following these instructions, will prepare a famous pudding for your dinner or supper. First, fry the birds whole with a little butter, shallot, parsley, thyme, and winter savory, all chopped small, pepper and salt to season; and when the birds are half done, shake in a small handful of flour, add rather better than a gill of water, stir the whole on the fire while boiling for ten minutes, and when the stew of birds is nearly cold, pour it all into a good-sized pudding basin, which has been ready-lined with either a suet and flour crust, or else a dripping-crust, cover the pudding in with a piece of the paste, and either bake or boil it for about an hour and-a-half.

From *Plain Cookery for the Working Classes* by
Charles Elmé Francatelli, London, 1852

However, the hedgerow is a rich source for the housewife in these difficult times. To the uninitiated, the idea of making soup f... collection, are off-putting and yet undeservedl...

Wha saw the tattie-howkers?
  Wha saw them gaun awa'?
Wha saw the tattie-howkers
  Sailing frae the Broomielaw?
Some o' them had boots an'
    stockin's,
  Some o' them had nane ava;
Some o' them had umbrellas,
  For to keep the rain awa'.

Grow Your Own
H E R B S

R O S E M A R Y   B U R N E T

Luntie Home Farm
10 miles north of Auchentogle

...a good medicine for ailing poultry is believed
to be nothing but an "old wives' tale."

SAGE. Perennial. One of the most useful
herbs, to be raised from seeds sown in April or
cuttings in late summer, the latter to be inserted
in sandy soil till well rooted. Sage thrives best
on a dry, sunny bank, and the bushes may be
trimmed to shape in the late summer.

Sage is used largely in stuffing and for sauces.
Leaves may be dried in summer, and then broken
up and stored for winter use, a glass receptacle with
a tightly-fitting lid being the best form of storage.

SAVORY. There are two varieties, the Summer
(a hardy annual) and the Winter (a perennial).
Both are used for salads and soups and for boiling
with peas and beans to improve the flavour.
Winter savory is best propagated by means of slips
or cuttings.

SORREL. Perennial. Simple to raise from seed
sown in May, or from divisions of established roots
in late summer. The plants should stand about
15 in. apart, and the leaves are much used with
soups and sauces. Sometimes sorrel and spinach
are served together as a dish.

SOUTHERNWOOD. Sometimes known as Lads'
Love, this perennial shrub should figure in a herb
corner for its perfume.

TANSY. Perennial. With its deep-green leaves
and small yellow flowers the plant is distinctly
ornamental. The foliage is used both for garnishing
and for the flavouring of cakes and puddings; whilst
tansy tea is still made in some parts as a medicine.
The plants should stand at least 2 ft. apart.

TARRAGON. Perennial. Best obtained by root
division or from cuttings. Much used for salads
and also as a flavouring when making pickles.

THYME. Perennial. The best garden variety
is Lemon Thyme, which does not seed, so that
propagation is effected by root division, preferably
in the early spring. Likes sandy soil and a dry,
sunny position. Other kinds of thyme may be
raised from seed sown in the late spring.

Sprigs of thyme may be dried in the height of
summer and stored for winter use, preferably in
glass jars with tightly-fitting stoppers.

2. THE CULTURE OF FRUIT

EVEN in comparatively small gardens there are
opportunities for growing fruit profitably,
but the soil must first be carefully prepared and
trees and bushes of the correct form and variety
selected, planting being done in such a way that

...e other occupants of the garden are not adversely
...ected either by shade from the thick foliage or
...poverishment from roots. Even in towns fruit is
...te within the bounds of possibility—a statement
...which there is abundant evidence.
...s a general rule, fruit is not recommended as a
...ure of a vegetable garden. A wiser plan is to
...ote one plot solely to fruit, though certain
...tch-crops" of vegetables may be grown between
...rows of bushes, just as a strawberry-bed may
...ure among vegetables. It is a question mainly
...lanning out one's plot so that there is one section
...fly for fruit, a second section for vegetables, and
...rd as the flower and pleasure part.
...the same time, to thrifty gardeners, the walls

A HALF STANDARD APPLE TREE, as recommended
for large gardens. Such trees should be planted
at intervals of 20 ft.

of the house, and even the sides of fences, may be
put to profitable use under sound management,
but the various points of site, aspect, and so on are
dealt with fully under the respective headings below.

APPLE. One of our most valuable fruits and
known to embrace nearly two thousand distinct
varieties. Among the forms in which young apple
trees may be purchased from nurserymen are the
following:

STANDARDS. Trees with main stems about 6 ft.
in height with bushy heads. Suitable for planting
at intervals of 25 ft. or 30 ft. (according to habit
and variety) in an orchard. Not suitable for a
comparatively small garden, except perhaps as an
isolated specimen in a roomy corner.

HALF-STANDARDS. Trees of similar shape but
with a main stem only 4 ft. 6 in. in length or slightly

Herb Vinegars

Wash and dry a good quantity of freshly gathered young shoots of whichever herb you are wanting to flavour the vinegar with, and put them into wide-necked bottles or jars. Cover with vinegar, seal, infuse for two months, then strain into small bottles, seal, and keep in a cool, dark place.

Pick the herb from the garden on a dry day before the plants begin to flower.

Herbs you could use in this way are mint, tarragon, thyme, dill, rosemary (bruise the rosemary a wee bit first), really, any herb that would be guid an' tasty in a salad dressing or a marinade.

Granpaw's Wine Making Tips

* Buy an expert's book on winemaking an' study up. I'm nae expert, just a gifted amateur!
* The best wine is made fae fruit you gether for free — it disna really taste ony better than bought stuff, it just seems that way cause ye never paid for it.
* Dinna expect miracles. This can be hit an' miss. Learn fae yer mistakes an' mind ye are trying tae mak' somethin' tasty — no' trying tae win ony prizes. Get recipes aff o' folk and ask their advice. Watch oot though, tae mak' the best wine ye need accurate instructions.
* You need equipment. A fermentation bucket wi a lid, a water-lock fermentation cork, a couple o' demijohns, some funnels, some big jaurs, siphon tubes, wine bottles, bottle cleaner and corks.
* The ingredients you need in stock are yeast, yeast nutrient, pectic enzyme, acid blend, Campden tablets and wine finings.
* Fruit has natural yeasts on the skin which might battle with added yeast, so wash it thoroughly. However, some wines use these natural yeasts alone in the fermentation process.
* Maist fruit needs tae be crushed first. Dinna use your feet tae crush the fruit, no matter whit ye've seen on the telly! A tattie champer or a food processor will do.
* Equipment needs to be thoroughly sterilised.
* Let the fruit and pulp and liquid sit for 24 hours in a warm place before you add yeast. Use a fermentation bag to collect the fruit pulp in, then put it back in the tub.
* Put yeast on the liquid surface and cover it. Sometimes the recipe will tell ye tae activate the yeast first (wi' sugar, water and warmth) and float it on top. I hae a few recipes whaur ye spread fresh yeast on toast and float it on the top. It micht tak' a day or twa afore the yeast starts to work. Once it starts working gie it a stir every day. Let the mixture ferment for aboot seven days and then scoop aff the scum (an' the toast), throw away the pulp and put liquid in a secondary fermenter wi' a water lock.
* Allow it tae ferment for aboot six weeks or until clear.
* Siphon it intae a clean demijohn and add finings.
* Bottle it an' age it. Some wines need tae sit a year or twa.
* Drink sensibly!

Wines, Drinks an' Syrups

A lot o' the ingredients for these can be gathered frae the wild tae. I love a bargain, especially when it's free! There are berries everywhere in late summer at the But an' Ben.

Ye can pick yer ain, grow yer ain an' find them in the wild. Granpaw can mak' wine oot o' onything, no' jist wi' berries — though I thought the turnip wine left a lot tae be desired!

Hame-made wines an' beers are as alcoholic as bought yins, sometimes mair sae. So treat them wi' respect and dinna overindulge! That means _you_ Hen.!!

Whit? I resent that remark!

Rosehip Syrup

Rosehips are ripe and ready to pick when they are bright red.

4 1/2 pts of water
2 lbs of rosehips
1 lb sugar

Wash the rosehips and cut off the tops and tails. Chop them in a food processor (you can chop them by hand but the wee hairy seeds will make your fingers itchy!). Boil 3 pints of water, add the chopped rosehips and continue to let it boil for half an hour. Remove from heat and leave to cool (about 15 minutes).

Strain through a jelly bag or muslin. Put the pulp from the jelly bag back in the pan and add 1 1/2 pints more boiling water. Stir well, then strain again. Combine the two lots of liquor in a clean pan. Boil to reduce the liquid to around 1 1/2 pints. Add the sugar and boil for 5 minutes. Sterilise some small jars or bottles in the oven and pour in the hot syrup.

Preserved Roses

1 lb red rose buds
4 quarts water
3 lb sugar
1 lemon, juice of

Take red rose buds clipped clean from their green parts. Put them into a skillet with four quarts of water, then let them boil very fast till three quarts are boiled away. Then put in three pounds of fine sugar, and let it boil till it begins to be thick, then put in the juice of a lemon, and boil it a little longer, and when it is almost cold, put it into sterilised jam jars.

Syrup of Roses
(or of any other flower)

Fill a glass basin three quarters full of spring water, then fill it up with rose-leaves or any other, and cover it, and set it inside a pot of simmering water one hour, then strain it, and put in more; and do in like manner, and so do seven times, then take to every pint one pound of Sugar, and make a syrup therewith.

FROM
TO

mint leaves
dissolve 1 lb. sugar in half pint water bring slowly to boil simmer for 20 mins. Remove from heat pour syrup dish leave to cool Dip flowers leaves quickly into syrup shake off excess ~~press toss~~

| DATE | castor | sugar | AM | dry | PM |
| MESSAGE RECEIVED BY | rose petals |

Marigold Syrup

6 oz marigold petals
1 ½ pints o' water
1 lb o' sugar
The juice o' a lemon

Boil the water. Add the petals an' reduce tae around 1 pint. Tak' awa' frae the heat an' strain. Add the sugar an' lemon juice to the marigold water an' stir till the sugar is dissolved. Return tae the heat an' boil till liquid becomes syrupy. Pour into sterilised jars.

This is guid for a sair throat! An' it's tasty diluted as a drink.

Bramble Syrup
Pour on desserts or add to spirits and cocktail

3 cups sugar granulated sugar
2 cups water
4 cups brambles, washed

Put fruit and sugar in a large pan. Pour the water over and gradually dissolve the sugar on a medium heat. Bring to a boil. Stir frequently. When it reaches boiling point turn down to simmer for around 10 minutes. Allow to cool then strain through a jelly bag into a clean container. Chill and use within 7 days.

GINGER BEER PLANT RECIPE

THIS is actually a recipe for a yeast culture rather than a genuine yeast–bacteria, ginger beer "plant". A ginger beer "plant" is not a plant with leaves and roots, it is a gelatinous, symbiotic organism that you can't make – it has to be bought or passed from wine-maker to wine-maker and kept alive through feeding with sugar. Rationing of sugar during the war made the making of home-made ginger beer mostly die out in Britain, and the ginger beer plants with it. They can still be bought from specialists though, but try this first, it works very well and gives a tangy, pleasant result.

$\frac{1}{2}$ oz dried yeast
2 tsp sugar
2 tsp ground ginger
1 pint (previously boiled) lukewarm water

Put all of the above ingredients into a large bowl, cover with a tea towel, and put in a warm place. This is our yeast version of the "plant". Feed it for seven days, giving it a teaspoon of ginger and one of sugar every day. Then take:

The juice of 4 lemons
1 $\frac{1}{2}$ lbs sugar
2 pints boiling water

... and place in a large (8-pint) sterilised container and stir well till the sugar has dissolved. Then add 5 pints of cold water and stir. Then strain the plant through muslin into the big container. Leave for two hours, then bottle.

There is a danger of explosion with all home brewing so corks which can pop out under extreme pressure are safer on glass bottles than screw-tops which might make glass explode. These days you could put it in plastic pop bottles, three-quarters full (with all the air squeezed out, to allow for expansion) and keep them in a cool place. The beer should be ready after about a week. Take care when opening the bottles as the lids can fly right off when loosened. Don't ever point at the face. The beer is only very mildly alcoholic (about 1%) so is safe for children .

There will be sediment left on the muslin. It can be used again and again. You must add a pint of lukewarm (previously boiled) water, feed it with sugar again, in a warm place, for two weeks and then divide it in two and put each part in its own jar with a cup of lukewarm water. Why not share your yeast "plant" with a friend, and pass on the instructions too.

Orangeade

Three oranges
1 oz sugar
2 pints water

With a zester, peel off the rind of one orange — avoid getting any of the white pith. Put the rind into a jug. Squeeze the juice from the oranges, reserve and chill. Add one ounce of sugar (or Acacia honey), to 2 pints of boiling water, and pour over the orange rind. Cover the jug, and leave overnight. Strain and chill.

Add the chilled orange juice, mix well and serve with lots of ice on a hot day.

APPLE-WATER

4 apples
Quart water
A little sugar

Slice up thinly three or four apples without peeling them, and boil them in a very clean saucepan with a quart of water and a little sugar until the slices of apple are become soft; the apple water must then be strained through a piece of clean muslin, or rag, into a jug. This pleasant beverage should be drunk when cold.

GINGER BEER.

See
opposite
page to
explain
aboot
ginger
beer
"plants"

Feed the plant daily for one week with
one teaspoonful of ground ginger and
one teaspoonful of sugar.   At the end
of a week strain through a muslin.   To
the liquid, which should be placed in a
large bowl, add the juice of two lemons,
18 cups of water and three cups of sugar,
which must be melted in another four cups
of boiling water.   Bottle and keep for
one week before using.   Do not quite fill
the bottles.

Scrape the plant back from the muslin
into a jar and cover with four cups of
water.   Mix well and divide into two
jars.   To each jar add two teaspoonfuls
of ground ginger and then proceed to feed
the plant as before, passing on one **half**
to a friend.   When feeding the plant
each day do not stir.

The plant must be divided each week or
it will die.   Feed the plant on Monday
morning and bottle on Monday afternoon
or evening.

Orange Liqueur

4 seville oranges
10 oz white sugar
-/2 oz powdered cinnamon
1 bottle of French brandy.

With a zester, peel off the outside rind of
the oranges, and bruise it with a mortar
and pestle. Mix sugar, with powdered
cinnamon. Put this mixture along with the
bruised orange rind into a large jar. Pour
in the French brandy, and put a secure lid
on it. Shake it every other day for three
weeks. Leave in a dark place. At the end
of that time, strain it through muslin or a
jelly bag and pour into a clean bottle.

is it real beer
maw?
can we hae
some?

75

Birch Sap Wine

Collect in early March while sap is rising. Dinna collect much mair than twa pints o' sap per tree, in case you kill the tree. Choose larger silver birch trees and, a few feet off the ground, drill about an inch into the tree. Or drive a sharp pointed knife into the tree at an upwards angle, then lift it to make the hole bigger. Now cut a tap for the tree. Cut a birch twig about 5 inches long (or long enough to clear the base of the tree so that the sap can drip into a container). Slice the twig in half lengthways and slice a channel lengthways into the middle of one half. With cut edge facing downwards shove this into the hole (at an acute angle facing downwards) and above a bucket to collect the sap. Plug the hole with wood when finished.

8 pints birch sap
2 lb sugar
½ lb chopped raisins
Juice of 2 lemons
General purpose yeast

Boil the sap, add the sugar and simmer for 10 minutes. Put the raisins in a brewing bucket and add the boiling liquid and lemon juice. When it has cooled to blood temperature add 1 tsp yeast. Cover, Leave to ferment for three days. Strain into a demi-john with an air lock and leave till fermentation process is finished. Move to a clean jar and let sediment settle. Bottle and keep for at least a month before drinking.

Nettle Beer

An English recipe, it still works a treat wi' Scottish nettles tae. Granpaw says he mahs it because it is guid for his rheumatism. Aye, right.

It is!

2 lb young nettle tops
1 gallon water
8 oz brown sugar
¼ oz fresh yeast spread
    on a piece o' toast
¼ oz ground ginger

I make my elderberry wine using a bit o' toast tae! Folk dinna believe me but it works!

Use a guid large pot. Boil the nettles in the water for aboot half an hour. Strain an' keep the liquid. Add sugar tae the liquid an' stir till it has dissolved. Stir in the ground ginger. Pour mixture into a brewing container an' then spread the yeast on the toast an' float on the surface o' the liquid. Cover an leave for aboot three days at room temperature. Strain again an' put into sealable sterilised bottles. Drink efter aboot twa days. If keeping longer, mind that fermenting liquids can explode!

Sugarelly Water

When I wis a boy we made this in my gang hut (Granpaw's shed), on the fly.

Pure, hard liquorice (from the chemist)
A glass lemonade bottle
Tap water

Pit aboot three or fower sticks o' pure, hard liquorice in a glass lemonade bottle. Fill the bottle wi' water. Gie it a richt guid shake. (There will be a lot o' foam that you can sook oot o' the bottle!) Screw the top back on an' shake it again. Put in a dark place for aboot a week. Shake it regularly. Efter a week you'll hae Sugarelly Water — it should be nice an' black an' thick.

Guid for the digestion but never really as nice as you expect it to be!

Parsley Honey

Use this as you would honey. An alternative is to leave out lemon and add 1 tsp vinegar at the end of the process.

5 oz parsley, chopped
1 1/2 pints of water
1 lb of sugar
Juice of a lemon (or a tsp vinegar)

from Frances O'Brien

Boil the water. Add the chopped parsley and reduce to around 1 pint. Strain and reserve liquid. Add sugar and lemon juice to this and stir till sugar dissolved. Return to the heat and boil till liquid becomes syrupy. Pour into sterilised jars.

Bramble Wine

Time: fifteen days to ferment using natural fruit yeasts.

One pound of sugar to two pounds of brambles
A quarter of a pint of gin or brandy.

Cover a quantity of brambles with water in a pan, and simmer on the stove to draw the juice out.

Strain them through a sieve into a fermenting tub and leave the juice to ferment for fifteen days.

Afterwards add a pound of sugar to two quarts of juice, with a quarter of a pint of gin or brandy. When bottled, do not cork it too close.

TURNIP. wine fae Jim Brownlee

3 lbs TURNIPS (SNOWBALL).
1/2 lbs RAISINS.
1 lb WHEAT.
2 ORANGES.
2 LEMONS.
PECTIN ENZYME.
YEAST NUTRIENT
G7 YEAST.

needs aboot a gallon o water tae

3 lbs. SUGAR

TURNIPS CHOPPED FINE & BOILED FOR 15 mins. (UNTIL VERY SOFT.), THEN STRAINED INTO PAIL. ADD LIQUIDISED RAISINS — ORANGES — LEMONS. BOIL WHEAT FOR 10 mins & ADD TO MIXTURE.

WHEN COOL ADD ENZYME AFTER 24 HRS ADD NUTRIENT — YEAST.

LEAVE FOR 5 DAYS. STRAIN & PLACE IN FERMENTATION VESSEL.

Turnip Wine

4 lbs turnips
3 lbs sugar
1 lemon
1 orange
1 gallon water
1 tsp yeast nutrient
Wine yeast

Maw wasnae
that fussed
aboot this
ane, but it
disnae taste
o' neeps!!

Scrub turnips an' chop into wee pieces.
Boil in some water till soft. Strain
the liquor into a brewing bin wi' a
lid. Add sugar an' stir. When cool,
add lemon an' orange juice, yeast
nutrient an' yeast. Cover for four days
in a warm place an' stir occasionally.
Strain into a demijohn wi' an airlock.
Once fermentation stops, siphon into a
clean jar wi' an airlock. Leave for aboot
6 months, checking airlock every week
or twa. Bottle an' age for 12 months.

Damson Gin

1 lb damsons
6 ozs sugar
75cl bottle gin

Wash the fruit an' discard bruised or bad ones. Prick fruit wi' a fork an' put in a wide-necked bottle wi' a lid or stopper. Add sugar. Top jar up wi' gin tae the rim. Shake the jar every day. It will take a day or twa tae dissolve a' the sugar. Store in a dark place. Mature for a year. Strain an' bottle.

Sloe Gin

1 lb sloes
4 oz sugar
75cl bottle gin
1 teaspoon almond essence

Use the same method as for Damson gin but also add a wee teaspoon o' almond essence. Strain and bottle efter a year.

Elderflower 'champagne'

Pick on a dry, sunny day

10 flower heads, flowers only, no stalks
2 lemons, sliced
1 gallon water
1 ½ lbs sugar
1 teaspoon citric acid

Remove the green from the elderflower heads, it is bitter. Put them into a fermentation bucket with the sliced lemons, add the water and leave for 2 to 3 days with the lid on. Strain the liquid through sterilised muslin and add the sugar and citric acid. Stir until the sugar has dissolved and pour into bottles. Dinna screw the tops on too tightly for approximately 14 days. It should be drinkable for about three months. Watch out for exploding bottles!

Dinna throw the preserved sloes or damsons awa. Put them in a wide-necked jar, add a bottle of pale sherry, leave for three months, an' ye get delicious fruit-flavoured sherry.

Advocaat

fae Jean Brownlee

This is my Hogmanay tipple. I like it tae be made intae a wee snowball for The Bells.

6 eggs, beaten weel
1 lb caster sugar
2 (large) tins evaporated milk
The juice o' a whole plastic squeezy
   lemon (ye ken the yin I mean)
A gill o' brandy (or a splash mair tae yer ain
   taste)

Switch the whole lot together wi' a whisk or in a blender till sugar is dissolved. Pour into a big bottle or a jar wi' a lid an' keep refrigerated. Ye can let it age for 1 tae 2 weeks afore ye drink it.
   Drink wi' lime cordial an' lemonade an' ye've got a snowball!

SCOTMARK

LEADER
18 lb

...et
...D LEADER
...op to length

Size 2

TROUT FISHING

AUCHENTOGLE & DISTRICT

Snechty river & Loch Luntie

Permit prices - see reverse

POCKET GUIDE

TO ACCOMPANY

ORDNANCE MAP

OF THE

AUCHENTOGLE

AREA

Note about Hardgraft's Sherry: Jimmy Brownlee's pal gied me this (Hardgraft wisna the maist industrious o' sorts, hence the nickname, but he made braw wine).
The instructions are a bit on the spare side but it makes a braw sweet strong sherry. Use guid, sweet, fresh grapes that hae a guid crunch. I like red grapes for this the best. Add boiling water tae the fruit, raisins, sugar an tatties, but dinna add ony yeast tae the next day.

HARDGRAFTS SHERRY

½ LB BLACK GRAPES
½ " RAISINS
2 " DEMERARA SUGAR
4 PINTS BOILING WATER
½ OZ YEAST
3 POTATOES CHIPPED
CHOP RAISINS CRUSH
GRAPES BOIL WATER
PUT SUGAR IN
BASIN THREE WEEKS
STRAIN + FILTER

Blackcurrant Liqueur
(or Crème de Cassis)

1 lb blackcurrants (frozen ones are fine)
Approx 2 oz sugar
A cinnamon stick
A couple of cloves
75 cl bottle of vodka (or another spirit)

Carefully remove all stalks. Pierce the skin of each berry several times with a needle. Put in a glass or earthenware jar with a sealable lid. Cover the berries with the sugar. Add the cinnamon stick and cloves and all of the vodka. Shake the jar every day till the sugar is dissolved. Keep in a dark cupboard for about three months. Taste and add more sugar if you think it needs it. Best matured for at least 6 months.

Blackberry W...
cover fruit wi...
water. Stand...
48 hrs. Bring t...
boiling fit ...
strain...
To each quart...
liquid add 1½ t...
of sugar a litt...
each day for 7 d...
stirring often...
Bottle but do...
not screw cor...
down for some ti...

Elderflower Wine

Elderflowers are in blossom between May
and July. Pick on a dry, sunny day.
Shake the flowers frae the stems intae a
bucket or pick them aff by hand – dinna
use the green stems.

1 pint o' elderflowers
Rind an' juice o' 1 lemon
1 gallon boiling water
3 lbs sugar
1 packet wine yeast
1 teaspoon yeast nutrient

In a large sterilised tub, or crock, place
the grated lemon rind, lemon juice an' the
elderflowers, 1 lb o' sugar, an' pour boiling
water over them. Cover an' leave tae
stand for 4 days, stirring occasionally.
   Strain through a sterilised muslin
cloth (I use Maw's guid clootie dumpling
cloth!). Stir in yeast nutrient an' yeast.
   Keep in a warm place (like an airing
cupboard) for three days. Strain into a
demijohn tae which has already been added
the remaining sugar. Put in an airlock
cork. Let it sit for three months an'
then siphon intae a clean demijohn. Leave
in a warm place till it no longer bubbles,
then bottle and mature for three months

83

Rumtopf

As fruits come intae season, I add them tae my Rumtopf! Mak' it in summer tae drink in the winter. I use a big tall glass jar wi' a lid on it. It hauds aboot fower quarts. This turns oot different for me every year, but it is aye guid as a wee hot toddy, on a cauld winter night.

Soft fruits as they come into season
Sugar
About 2 quarts o' rum

Here's a typical summer's Rumtopf: Start aff wi' strawberries an' raspberries, cover in an equal weight o' sugar, e.g. 1 lb fruit tae 1 lb sugar. Cover entirely wi' rum tae about twa inches above. Cover wi' a lid an' place at the back o' a cool cupboard. Stir it every three or fower days.

Later on, goosberries will come in tae season, so I add a cup o' them but only half their weight in sugar, an' fill up tae cover completely wi' mair rum. Later on I'll get a few brambles, half their weight in sugar an' add mair rum. Repeat wi' fruits as they come intae season an' till the Rumtopf jar is fu'. Shake or stir every twa weeks. Leave for a couple o' months. At end o' November, taste an' add mair rum if required (if ye think it is a bit too sweet for instance).

By December it will be ready. A lovely drink for the lassies tae see in The Bells wi'! Strain an' decant into bottles. Use the preserved fruit for puddings: lovely wi' vanilla ice cream!

85

SCOTMARK

LEADER
18 lb

...et
...D LEADER
...oop to length

Size 2

TROUT FISHING

AUCHENTOGLE & DISTRICT

*Snechty river
& Loch Luntie*

Permit prices - see reverse

POCKET GUIDE

TO ACCOMPANY

ORDNANCE MAP

OF THE

AUCHENTOGLE

AREA

Seaside Pichic Checklist

Fishing nets
Bucket and spade
fitba
windbreak
cagoul

Wellies
Tent
Towels
Trunks
suncream

no TRIP is complete Unless sandy
legs and feet skelped clean by maw
slapping The sand aff them. OW!

Fish van passes on
Thursdays, stops
at 11am at the
end o' the lane.
Be waiting for
him or he'll go by!

Catch o' The Day

We've had some braw days oot by the
river an' at the seaside. An' even if
we dinna manage tae catch oorsels a
wee fishy there's a guid fishmonger
in Auchentogle an' a chippy wi' the
best fish suppers in Scotland. When
Paw was a boy he used tae guddle
for fish in the Snechty River.

Finnan Haddie an' Rice

Braw comfort food. The best smoked haddocks are frae Green's fishmongers in Auchentogle. Paw an' Granpaw tried smoking their ain last year. Oh dear.

Groo! – what a richt pair o' haddies!

2 ozs long grain rice
1 large fillet o' Finnan haddie
Milk (about half a pint or mair)
Salt an' pepper
1 oz butter
1 oz flour

Boil the rice. Poach the fish in enough milk tae cover it, an' add salt an' pepper an' the butter. Strain aff the milk an' keep it. Remove skin an' bone fae the haddie, an' flake the fish.

Mak a white sauce wi' the butter, flour, an' the milk fae the haddie.

Dish up the fish on top o' the rice, an' pour the sauce ower it.

white sauce recipe on page 98

Potted Herring

2 fresh herrings
salt and pepper
1/4 pint water
1/4 pint wine vinegar
1 teaspoon brown sugar
1 bay leaf
8 black peppercorns
1 onion, sliced finely

Clean and bone the herrings, season with salt and pepper and place in a pie dish. Boil the vinegar and water with the sugar, bay leaf and onions and simmer tae let out the flavours. Strain and pour this liquid over the fish. Bake for about an hour. Serve cold.

Fishcakes

1/2 oz. butter
1 dessertspoon milk
1/2 lb mashed potato
1lb flaked cooked fish
one well-beaten egg
pepper and salt

Melt the butter in the milk; add potato and fish, and beat well over slow heat. Allow to cool for a little, add the egg and seasonings. Form into cakes and finish like croquettes.

Soused Mackerel
Serves two

2 fresh mackerel fillets·
Enough vinegar and water (in equal amounts) to cover them.
2 garlic cloves, crushed
1 small onion, finely sliced
1 bay leaf,
6 peppercorns,
1 teaspoon salt.

Roll up the fish and secure with a cocktail stick. Put in a deep oven dish with a lid with vinegar, water, garlic and other seasonings. Cover the dish. Bake for an hour in a moderate oven.

Tatties an' Herring

This is a quid one-pot dinner. I've no' gied quantities, but, for instance, ye could hae twa herrin' an' three tatties each. Judge fae that.

Herring
Tatties
Salt
Pepper
Water
Butter
Rolled oats

Peel some tatties an' cover wi' water. Bring tae the boil, an', when the tatties are half-cooked, pour aff maist o' the water. Return the pot tae the heat, place the herring ower the tatties, cover closely, an' cook in the steam. Lift the fish on tae a plate an' keep warm, an' steam the tatties till dry and floury. Then add butter an' sprinkle the tatties wi' some rolled oats, an' dish up wi' the fishies.

91

FROG SOUP
5 LIVE FROGS
3 LIVE baggie minnows
A bucket o' RIVER WATER

Serve STRAIGHT fae The
bucket Tae Granpaw. He
says he likes his fish VERY
fresh.

Sweet Peppers Stuffed with Crab

The meat of 2 crabs
⅓ cup breadcrumbs
2 tbsps melted butter.
1 small onion, chopped and fried
2 slightly beaten eggs
Pepper, salt
Juice of half a lemon

Mix all the ingredients, season well.
Cut off the tops of six red or
green peppers, remove the insides.
Put crab mixture into peppers;
sprinkle crumbs on top, and bake
in the centre of the oven at 375°F
for 10 minutes.

NAPKIN BROLLY

HERE'S a pretty and really
new idea in table decoration
—a napkin made into an
umbrella.
To make this napkin umbrella all
you need is a lemonade straw, a
pipe-cleaner and a paper napkin.
Take a napkin and fold it in half.
Slide pipe-cleaner through
lemonade straw so that about 1in. of cleaner
juts out from one end. Curve this into a handle.
Slip the umbrella stick into the centre of the
opened out napkin

OGDEN SMITHS Ltd.

62, ST. JAMES'S STREET,
PICCADILLY, LONDON, S.W.1

Fishing Tackle
Manufacturers

Telephone & Telegrams
REGent 2612

REVISED PRICES

SALMON RODS

"WARRIOR" Double built bamboo, 12 sections
2 or 3 joints   extra top joint

9 ft.	10 ft.	11 ft.	12 ft.	13 ft.	14 ft.
£9-9-0	£10-10-0	£11-11-0	£12-12-0	£13-13-0	£14-14-0

For Fly or Bait Spinning, same prices

SALMON REELS

"SEPARA"	-	4 inch 70/-	4½ inch 84/-
"REALM"	-	4 inch 50/-	4½ inch 63/-

SALMON LINES

"OILEVEL"
No. 4 40/-   No. 5 45/-   No. 6 50/-   Per 50 yards
Tapered line not available

SALMON CASTS

Sizes:	8/5	7/5	6/5	5/5	4/5	3/5	2/5	1/5
3 yards -	3/6	4/6	5/6	7/6	10/6	15/6	21/-	25/-
2 " -	2/6	3/-	3/9	5/-	7/-	10/6	15/-	17/6

"MERMAID" SALMON FLIES

Sizes:	10	9	8	7	6	5	4	3	2
Prices -	1/2	1/4	1/6	1/9	2/-	2/3	2/6	2/9	3/-

Sizes :	1	1/0	2/0	3/0	4/0	5/0	6/0	7/0	8/0
Prices -	3/3	3/6	3/9	4/-	4/3	4/6	5/-	5/6	6/-

LOW WATER FLIES

Size : 9—1/4, 8—1/6. 7—1/8, 6—1/10

PRESERVED BAITS

Prawns, Sprats, Minnows, from 3/-

CASTING BAITS, DEVONS, PHANTOMS, SPOONS, from 1/-

THE WAR AND FISHING TACKLE

Most of the fishing tackle shops are empty.
We had enormous stocks when war broke out,
we continued to supply at pre-war prices, no
purchase tax. We regret the present advance, of
which we have no control. Many lines are coming
to an end, such as Reels, Lines, Cases, Boxes and
Accessories. Rods are few, Gut casts better, Flies
the best. We still have the best and largest stocks
in the world. Specials are out of the question, our
works almost entirely devoted to war work, our
staff depleted, so please allow for short comings
and delays.

PERSONAL—In reply to many enquiries, the 3 sons (Directors) who left
before the declaration for the Army, are safe and well, after Dunkirk,
Bardia, Crete, etc. They tender their thanks and hope soon to be back
again amongst the tackle.

92

Popular Edition
ONE-INCH MAP
of SCOTLAND
AUCHENTOGLE & DISTRICT

SHEET 48B

Price (Paper) Two Shillings Net

Cod

Fried Cod Fingers

For the batter:
5 oz self-raising flour
About 2 tbsps malt vinegar
8 fl oz beer (or fizzy water)

2 large fillets o' cod
1 cup o' oil an' vinegar seasoned wi'
  chopped onion an' parsley.
Batter, or egg an' breadcrumbs

Cut the fillets into pieces the width o'
twa fingers an' lay for an hour in oil
an' vinegar. Drain, dry, dip in batter or
egg an' breadcrumbs an' deep fry.

Baked Cod

2 large fillets o' cod
1 cup o' breadcrumbs, seasoned wi'
  pepper, salt, an' parsley
2 slices o' bacon
A lemon

Grease a deep oven dish, lay in one fillet,
add half the crumbs, an' sprinkle some
lemon juice ower it. Lay on, first the
other fillet, then more crumbs, an'
lastly the slices o' bacon.
  Cover wi' foil an' bake for half an hour
in a fairly hot oven. Serve wi' chopped
fresh tomatoes.

TROUT TICKLING or, as the pratice is better known in Scotland, "guddling", is the riverside art of rubbing the underside of a trout using the fingers with the intention of lulling it into a trance-like condition. The practitioner lies on his stomach at the river's edge with hands dangling in the water to wait for a trout to pass. The trout is then tickled till in a trance and then thrown (carefully) on to the riverbank. Poachers liked this method as no equipment was needed. It was also a common activity during times of economic hardship such as the 1930s.

"The fish are watched working their way up the shallows and rapids. When they come to the shelter of a ledge or a rock it is their nature to slide under it and rest. The poacher sees the edge of a fin or the moving tail, or maybe he sees neither; instinct, however, tells him a fish ought to be there, so he takes to the water very slowly and carefully and stands up near the spot. He then kneels on one knee and passes his hand, turned with fingers up, deftly under the rock until it comes in contact with the fish's tail. Then he begins tickling with his forefinger, gradually running his hand along the fish's belly further and further toward the head until it is under the gills. Then comes a quick grasp, a struggle, and the prize is wrenched out of his natural element, stunned with a blow on the head, and landed in the pocket of the poacher."

Thomas Martindale, Sport, 1901

What is the best way to avoid sunburn in the summer in Scotland?

Just keep your hat cagoul and wellies on.

Brown Trout

There is guid eating in brown trout, probably at its best in May.

Wash in cold water. Ye dinna hae to scale them: gut, clean, an' dry the fish. Dip it in cauld watter an' then in oatmeal, an' fry in butter in a frying pan, an' dish up wi' a squeeze o' lemon.

In the unlikely event that Paw brings hame a huge trout that canna be cooked in the frying pan, ye can cook them in the oven tae. Put into a buttered oven dish. Cover wi' chopped onion, an' chopped parsley, add dry white wine an' a drappie butter. Cover with a lid or with foil, an' bake in a moderate oven for 20 tae 25 minutes.

FLY CASTING NO "MYSTERY" ABOUT IT......
ONCE YOU UNDERSTAND THE SIMPLE PRINCIPLES

Make no mistake, average-to-good fly casting does NOT take weeks of practice or require you to develop some mystic sense of handling and timing. It's really simple, once you realize that it isn't really the fly you're casting; it's the line. The weight of the line, when cast behind you, bends the rod... and then the power of the rod, as activated by your forearm, drives the line out forward, taking some more line with it. Even a few minutes of practice, following the suggestions below, will give you the "feel" of it. Accuracy and control will come later — as you fish.

TAKE UP SLACK FIRST
Stretch out 25 to 30 feet of line. Holding line in left hand, take up slack and start cast with rod at about two o'clock position.

PICK UP SMARTLY······AND AIM HIGH
With a sharp upward stroke, aim to send the lure high and to the rear. Line should form a loop that quickly straightens out behind you. Stop rod at twelve o'clock.

WAIT FOR 'PULL' AT ROD TIP
As the loop straightens out, your rod will drift back from 'twelve' and you'll feel a slight pull at the tip — and on the line held in your left hand.

MAKING THE FORWARD CAST
The instant the loop straightens out behind you, start the forward cast······ exactly like the back cast. Stop the rod at two o'clock.

READY FOR THE STRIKE!
Now, let the line shoot through the left hand. Rod drifts down as line shoots out. As lure touches the water, gather any slack in your left hand, ready for action!

Baked Perch

Paw an' Granpaw sometimes manage tae catch a few wee perch an', noo an' then, we have eaten them cooked in butter. Wee anes taste nicest. They cook weel wi' a bit o' cream tae.

2 lbs o' perch
2 onions, chopped
1 leek chopped
2 tablespoons butter
1 teaspoon salt
½ cup single cream
Some grated cheese
2 tablespoons lemon juice
½ teaspoon paprika
Fresh chopped parsley

Fry the onion an' leek slowly in butter until soft an' sweet. Spread them ower the bottom o' a baking dish. Put the fish on top. Mix the cream, cheese, lemon juice, an' paprika together an' pour it ower the fish. Bake at 250°F for about half an hour. Sprinkle wi' chopped parsley. Serves 6.

White Sauce

2 oz butter
2 oz flour
1 pint liquid (milk, water, or
  fish or meat stock)

Melt the butter in a saucepan.
Add the flour, mix thoroughly
and cook for a few minutes.
Add liquid gradually, beating
well, add seasoning; stir till
boiling point, cook five minutes,
or until the flour is a' cooked
out.

Macaroni & Fish Pie

3 oz macaroni
One good-sized
  filleted smoked
  haddock
1 pint white sauce
Pepper and salt
Breadcrumbs
Butter

Cook the macaroni
in plenty o' boiling
salted water, drain it
well. Make the sauce,
add the macaroni, the
fish — cut up small
and the seasoning.
  Pour into a pie dish,
or pyrex, sprinkle
with breadcrumbs
and pats o' butter,
and bake, in a
moderate oven, fifteen
to twenty minutes.

FISHING PERMIT

AUCHENTOGLE
& DISTRICT
SUMMER SEASON

August 6 — August 15

£3
PAID   James McTavish

On behalf of:
Auchentogle & District Fisheries Board

98

Mussels

We hae quite plain taste in the Broon family so ye micht think that mussels widnae be my thing. But, feeling adventurous, I once tried them at Jeannie Aberdour's Seafood Café in Auchentogle an', oh! they were braw!

2 lbs mussels
1 onion, finely
  chopped
1 clove garlic, crushed
Fresh parsley

Dry white wine
Butter
A guid glug o'
  cream
Salt an' pepper

Scrub mussels, tae get rid o' beards an' barnacles. Fry onions in butter till soft. Add garlic, black pepper, about 5 fl oz o' wine an' bring tae the boil. Throw mussels in liquid an' boil, covered, for 2 minutes. Check an' stir. After another 2 minutes check again – discard unopened mussels. Put mussels in a warm dish. Keep cooking liquor an' strain it (it may be gritty). Return tae pan, add butter, cream, parsley an' simmer. Pour ower mussels. Serves twa people.

Shouldna say this, but if ye're feeling lazy ye can jist bung scrubbed mussels intae a big pan on their ain and they will cook in their ain juice aince the shells have opened. Couldna be easier!

Lemon Sole in Lemon an' Dill

Lemon sole is best frae December tae March. So that's something tae look forward tae in the winter!

3 tablespoons o' butter
Finely chopped fresh dill (check Granpaw's herb patch)
1 tablespoon lemon juice
1/4 teaspoon salt
1 large onion, finely chopped
2 fillets o' lemon sole

Heat butter in a large, wide pan wi' a lid over a low heat an' slowly soften the onions. When soft add the fresh dill, lemon juice an' salt. Add the fillets, mak' sure they are a' weel covered in the butter an' onions. Cover an' cook for about 10 minutes, checking regularly. Serves twa fowk.

LUNTIE LOCH
FLY SELECTION

FROM THE AUCHENTOGLE FILLING STATION

HOOK 10 SIZE

Baked Carp

A 1-lb carp
1 large onion, finely chopped
2 tbsps fresh parsley, chopped
Cooking oil
Lemon juice
Salt

Gut and clean carp. Cut into steaks. Mix onion, parsley and oil. Make holes in the steaks with a sharp pointed knife. Rub onion mixture all over and force in the holes. Put in an oiled baking dish. Sprinkle with salt and give them all a good squeeze of lemon juice. Bake at 350° F. for about 30 minutes or until done. (Roast some parboiled potatoes with oil, salt and chopped rosemary at the same time as you bake the fish.)

FISH IN SEASON

JANUARY	FEBRUARY	MARCH	APRIL	MAY	JUNE	JULY	AUGUST	SEPTEMBER	OCTOBER	NOVEMBER	DECEM
Cod	Cod	Halibut	Brown trout	Brown trout	Brown trout	Bass	Bass	Bass	Bass	Bass	Bass
Haddock	Haddock	Mussels	Crab	Crab	Crab	Crab	Crab	Cod	Cod	Cod	Cod
Halibut	Halibut	Oysters	Halibut	Haddock	Bass	Bass	Haddock	Halibut	Haddock	Haddock	Haddock
Mussels	Mussels	Scallops	Mussels	Mussels	Haddock	Haddock	Halibut	Haddock	Halibut	Halibut	Halibut
Oysters	Oysters	Sole, Lemon	Oysters	Prawns	Lobster	Halibut	Lobster	Lobster	Mackerel	Mackerel	Mussels
Scallops	Scallops	Shrimps	Sea trout	Sea trout	Prawns	Lobster	Mackerel	Mackerel	Mussels	Mussels	Oysters
Turbot	Turbot		Prawns	Salmon	Salmon	Prawns	Prawns	Mussels	Prawns	Oysters	Scallops
Sole, Dover	Sole, Dover		Shrimps	Shrimps	Sea trout	Salmon	Sole, Dover	Prawns	Oysters	Sole, Dover	Sole, D
Sole, Lemon	Sole, Lemon		Lobster	Lobster	Sole, Dover	Sea trout	Salmon	Oysters	Shrimps		Turbot
					Shrimps	Shrimps	Shrimps	Shrimps	Sole, Dover		
						Turbot	Turbot	Turbot	Turbot		
								Sole, Dover			

Dover Sole

Dover sole is a braw bit o' fish, available maist o' the year. This recipe is a wee bit fancier than I usually cook an' I dinna tell Paw there's anchovies in it. It gies me an' excuse tae open a wee bottle o' red wine tae.

2 soles
3 tablespoons butter
2 or 3 bay leaves
White pepper
Black pepper
2 cups red wine
2 anchovies, chopped finely
Some lemon juice

Melt the butter in a big frying pan. Put the bay leaves an' pepper in the melted butter an' leave it tae infuse for about an hour. Scale an' clean the soles. Place in an oven dish. Pour the herby melted butter over the fish an' then the red wine, an' then add the anchovies. Cook in the centre of the oven at 350°F till tender (which should be around 30 minutes).

WONDER BITES

4 oz. icing sugar
3 oz. coconut
2 oz. chopped cherries
6 oz. cooking choc.

2 oz. marg.
2 oz. marshmallows
1 teasp. coffee essence
   or liquid coffee

Cream fat, sugar and add cherries, marshmallows and coffee
etc.   Make into balls and dip in melted choc.

MALLOW DELIGHTS

4 oz. choc.

butter
rge tabsp. icing
gar

dd yolks.   Add
.   Add chopped
s and dip in

----

white sugar
salt.

Press into

----

conut

lted choc.

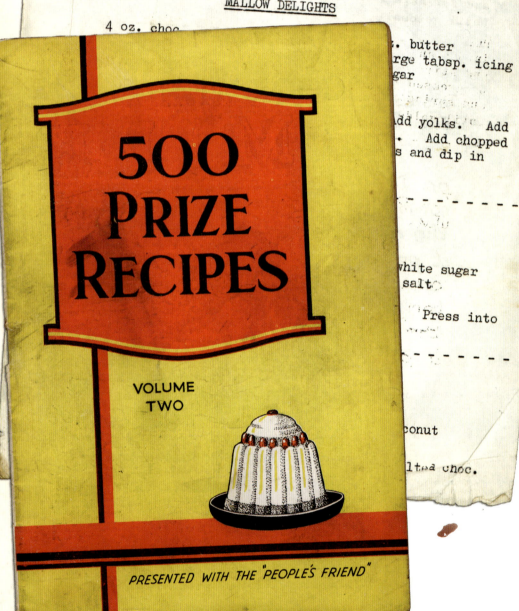

Prize Cooking

I dinna mean tae blow my ain trumpet but I've had some success at highland shows an' S.W.R.I. fêtes wi' some o' these.

The But an' Ben is really too wee for doing loads o' baking an' the oven is a bit temperamental so it's only really at competition season that I do that much baking. I can aye stick a clootie dumplin' in the big pot though!

Victoria Sponge

This is the sponge we mak' in the S.W.R.I. "cook-offs". The mixing an' temperature are crucial. A bit difficult at the But an' Ben — that cooker has a mind o' its ain!

6 oz unsalted butter
6 oz caster sugar
6 oz self-raising flour
3 eggs
1 tsp vanilla essence
Double cream
Strawberry jam (or raspberry jeely)
Icing sugar

Preheat oven tae 375 F, an' butter twa 8-inch sandwich tins. Sieve the flour onto a plate. In a large mixing bowl cream the butter an' sugar together until awfy pale and feuffy. Add the beaten eggs gradually an' mix thoroughly wi' an electric beater. Also add a little o' the sieved flour. Ye dae this tae stop the mixture curdling. Gently fold in the remaining flour an' add the vanilla. Divide between the sandwich tins an' bake for 20 tae 25 minutes. Turn oot ontae a wire rack tae cool. Fill wi' whipped cream, hame-made jam, an' dust wi' icing sugar.

109

Meringues – The Basics
Egg whites
Caster sugar (2oz for every egg white)

Use a totally grease-free glass or ceramic bowl (clean with vinegar or lemon juice to make sure). If any yolk gets in the white when you separate them your meringues won't work, so be careful. If you wish to avoid a chewy centre add 1/8 teaspoon of cream of tartar per egg white to unbeaten egg whites. (I like the chewy bit.) 2 egg whites will make about 6 meringues. Whip the egg whites to soft dry peaks. Use an electric mixer or you are in for a lot of work! Don't add the sugar till the eggs are properly whipped. Use no less than 2oz white sugar per egg white, then beat carefully to firm peaks. Wet (do not grease) a baking sheet and flour it. Pipe or spoon the mixture in round blobs onto the sheet. Bake at 200°F (100°C) for about 1½ hrs. Turn off oven but leave them in there overnight without opening the door.

Isa Brownlee's recipe

Swiss Tart Pastry.

½ lb. Pl. flour
½ a. butter
2oz. icing sugar
2oz. cornflour.

Rub all together thoroughly with the fingertips, then bind. Ye could use this Swiss tart pastry for the aipple pie — it is the best. Sadly, that is because it is the maist fattening.

Macaroons

4 3 Shortcrust pastry

Filling

2 Egg whites.
4 oz. sugar.
2 tablespoons Semolina or Farola.
A few drops almond essence.
Raspberry jam.

Beat egg white till stiff. Add almond essence. Mix sugar and semolina. Fold into egg white.
Bake mod oven for ½ hour.

110

Easy Peasy Almond Macaroons

—

1 cup ground almonds
¾ cup sugar
1 egg white (be prepared, you might need more depending on size of egg)
1/2 tsp. vanilla extract
some whole skinned almonds
Preheat oven to 400°F.

Gradually mix the egg white into the dry ingredients above, till mixture is thick and sticky and shapeable. Depends on the size of the egg, so judge as you go along. Each macaroon should be about the size of a walnut. Put on a baking tray covered in rice paper. Brush each one with some water. Put a whole almond on top of each one. Bake for 15 minutes.

American-Style Aipple Pie

I got this recipe fae Paw's Aunt Martha. There is a nine-inch pie tin for it inside the cooker.

Pastry:

2 cups plain flour
1 pinch salt
1 tablespoon sugar
6 tablespoons salted
  butter
6 tablespoons lard
6—8 tbsps cold water

Filling:

5 guid fresh cooking
  aipples
1 cup sugar
2 tablespoons flour
1/2 teaspoon cinnamon
1/4 teaspoon salt
1 tablespoon lemon juice

page 120 for hints on making guid pastry

Mix fat, salt an' flour tae breadcrumb consistency, then bind tae a firm dough wi' some water an' set aside tae cool an' rest. Peel an' slice aipples an' toss in lemon juice. In a large bowl, mix sugar, flour, spice an' salt. Mix the aipples wi' the dry mixture.

Cut the dough intae twa bits. Roll intae circles. Put ane on the bottom o' the pie tin. Prick a' ower wi' a fork. Pour in the filling (an' a few wee dods o' butter). Cover wi' pastry. Bake at 400°F for 50 minutes (the But an' Ben cooker aye burns the crust so cover the edges in tin foil till about 15 minutes afore the end). Serve hot wi' clotted cream fae Browning's Dairy.

111

SNOW BALLS.   10.

1 Cup Peanut Butter.   ½ cup Chopped Fruits.
   (raisins, dates cherries.)
½ cup chopped nuts.   1 cup Icing sugar.

Make into small balls and dip in thin butter icing.
Roll in Coconut or ground nuts or wafer crumbs.
If preferred dip in melted semi-sweet chocolate
with a little butter added and roll as above.

FAMILY GUIDE
TO THE

National Insurance

SCHEME

The Scheme comes into
full operation on

5th JULY 1948

PREPARED BY THE CENTRAL OFFICE OF INFORMATION FOR THE MINISTRY OF
NATIONAL INSURANCE AND PUBLISHED BY HIS MAJESTY'S STATIONERY OFFICE

AUCHENTOGLE
CHURCH

ng Wives & Mothers Group

Recipe Book

6d

Winter Whisky Marmalade

Made in summer for the winter '...
when Seville oranges are in season. They
dinna grow up here o' course but ye can
get them in the summer markets. This
matures nicely ower the months an' has
a guid sloosh o' malt whisky in it tae
help it alang. This is awfy hard an'
awfy hot work so I deserve a prize for it!

3 lbs Seville oranges
2 lemons
5 pints water
2 lb white sugar
2 lb brown sugar
'/4 pint malt whisky So that's whaur my guid malt
keeps disappearin' tae!

Ye'll need an awfy big jeely pan. Boil the
whole oranges an' lemons in water in the
pan, an' cover an' simmer for 3 hours.
Pour aff cooking water but keep it. Put
the fruit in a bowl tae cool. Return
cooking liquor tae pan. Cut oranges an'
lemons in half. Scoop oot flesh (discard

113 Continued
on page
after next

Date & wal...

1 cup Plain flour
1 " S.R. "
1 " sugar
2 or 3 dates
1 cup sultanas
Nuts
2 oz marg.   2 eggs
Steep dates & sultana...
with boiling water.
1 teaspoon spiced / gin...

Isa's Loaf

Isa Brownlee gied me this recipe. It's a lovely sweet, sconey loaf wi a nice sugary crust, that is braw sliced and spread wi butter. It's a renn easy ane tae mind because the measurements are 5,4,3,2,1. Use a 7 1/2-inch loaf tin.

5 tbsps self-raising flour
4 tbsps milk
3 tbsps sugar
2 oz butter
1 large egg
Caster sugar for the top

Sieve the flour. Mix the milk wi' the sugar and the egg. Melt the butter. Beat all together. Pour into greased loaf tin and sprinkle top wi' caster sugar. Bake at 350F for 30 minutes. Cool and serve in slices spread wi' butter.

Aunt Kate's RATION RECIPE BOOK

...fruit and quarter. Put stones
...uslin bag and steep with
...sugar overnight
...slowly till rolling then
...till thickens. batch at
...ckining

lemon peel but keep orange peel, pith and pips) an' set aside in a saucepan. Add pips an' pith tae the water in the jeely pan. Boil for 10 minutes an' strain through muslin, an' return liquor tae the pan again, still retaining the orange peel.

Add 1 pint o' the jeely pan liquor tae the fruit flesh in the saucepan. Simmer for 10 minutes. Strain into the pan through muslin,. Gie the muslin a guid hard squeeze.

Cut orange peel into thin strips. Watch ye dinna add too much pith. Add tae the pan. Heat the sugar in a warm oven for ten minutes. Add tae the pan an' stir. Slowly bring tae the boil.

Boil for 20 minutes or so until setting point is reached (test for a wrinkle on a cold plate). Add the whisky.

Tak' the pan aff the heat an' skim any scum frae the surface (a wee totie dod o' butter can help wi' this). Let it cool a little then pot in sterilised jars.

How Tae Mak Girdle Scones

Frae Grandmaw Broon

Anything that can be eaten hot aff a girdle will hae a'body slaverin'! I'm sure ye ken this, but a girdle is a strong, thick round o' iron, wi' a haundle across it, no' the knickers that haud yer belly in!

The girdle should be warm, but no' too hot, afore the scones are put on it. If ye haud yer haund aboot an inch abin it ye should feel a warm glow. Like I do efter a wee dram.

The proportions for plain scones are easy tae mind: 1 teaspoonful o' baking soda an' 1 teaspoonful cream o' tartar tae a pound o' plain flour.

Buttermilk is withoot a doubt best for plain scones, but if it is not tae be had, use milk, an' double the cream o' tartar tae mak' up for the lack o' auid. Stir buttermilk weel afore use.

Note!!: I won't gie a definite quantity o' milk for girdle scones. Add gradually till the dough is soft, but not wet.

Jist cooka few at a time till ye get the hang o' it — sometimes the first yin is the worst yin!

Plain Girdle Scones

This is an easy yin tae mind — think o' quarters o' a'thing! Oh ... apart fae the butter.

1/4 lb plain flour
1/4 teaspoon cream o' tartar
1/4 teaspoon baking soda
1/4 teaspoon sugar
1/4 teaspoon salt
1/2 oz butter
Buttermilk

Sieve the dry ingredients together. Rub the butter in with the fingers. Add the milk gradually, enough tae bring it together tae a soft and yet not wet dough.

Turn the dough onto a floured surface. Knead it lightly.

Roll out till about half an inch thick. Cut rounds wi' a scone cutter an' place on a warm, greased girdle. Turn to brown on baith sides. Bake the scones till weel risen an' a nice broon colour.

THE NUTHATCH

GROSSET'S FILTERLESS

Directions to Browning's Dairy.

Lovely cheese. And they will do you some nice yoghurt in a wee metal can - smashing with fresh rasps.

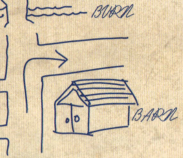

BURN

BARN

After the Sangster's barn, take a right turn after the second left turn on your way to the burn.

* If you see two oak trees and a hedgerow you've gone too far.

If so, go back and take a ~~right~~ left near two sycamores and go right past the grain silo at Watson's farm but not too far along or you'll reach Riley's farm and they'll set their dog on you.

You want to be turning right at the grain silo and along for a quarter of a mile and then take the third left after the first right after the second left near the bus stop.

Browning's Dairy.

You can't miss it!

Receipt to be sold
Money to be used fo

Milk less, eggless,

Ing. 2 cups flour
2 " Seede
1 " Wate
1 " Brow
1/3 " Lar
1 Tea Sp Cinn
1 " " noun
1/4 " " Nu
1 " " Soc
1/2 " " Ba
Pinch Salt.

Method
Boil all ing
+ baking powde
when cool ad
in a little hot
which the baking powde
been dytes.
Bake in a moderate to
One hour

Short Crust Pastry

Add a wee dash of sugar for sweet pies.

1 lb flour
8 oz butter, or butter and lard
1/2 teaspoon salt
Cold water (about 1 tbsp for every ounce flour)

Sieve the flour. Cut fat into cubes, add tae the flour and using awfy cold hands (chill them in cauld water if ye can) rub the fat into the flour tae mak' the mixture look like breidcrumbs. Add salt and sufficient cold water tae mak' a stiff dough. Roll out once. Dinna over handle your dough or allow tae get warm.

Australian Buns.

1/4 lb. Marg.
6 z. Flour (Plain)
3/4 Cup Sugar.
1 teaspoon Baking Powder.
1 Egg.
Fruit (half cup dried fruit)

Cream marg + sugar. Add egg. Add dry ingredients. Mix together Roll into balls and roll in wheat or corn flakes.

Bake mod. 350° oven for about 20 minutes. Till golden.

(Ruth Muir's recipe + handwriting)

Be-Ro Home Recipes

Scones, Cakes, Pastry, Puddings.

Beetroot Chutney

I got this recipe fae Margaret Purdie an' she got it fae Meg Thomson. It is simply the best beetroot chutney.

A little butter
1 lb onions, chopped
1lb cooking apples, chopped
½ lb sugar
3 ½ lbs beetroot (approx 3lbs after cooking and skinning)
1 pint vinegar
½ teaspoon salt
½ teaspoon ground ginger

Put raw beetroot in cold water in a big pot, bring tae the boil an' simmer till soft. Cool an' remove skins (ye can do this by rubbing wi' a cloth). Dice the beetroot or grate.
    Thoroughly clean a large pot. Melt a dod o' butter an' sweat chopped onions an' chopped cooking apple till soft. Add sugar an' then add beetroot. Pour vinegar over, add salt an' ginger an' simmer for about 20 minutes. Sterilise some jars by washing them an' then heating in a hot oven. Fill jars an' seal.

Cothall
Dundee Road
Coupar Angus
by Blairgowrie
4th September

Dear Mrs Brown

It was lovely to meet you at the S.W.R.L. fete last week. Your winning Beetroot Chutney was absolutely delicious and I was very grateful to you for letting me have a jar. I had some visitors at the weekend and they all commented on how tasty it was with our oatcakes and cheese after dinner.

I enjoyed your Victoria Sponge very much too. I was delighted that it won a joint first with my own but, perhaps, if I am honest, yours had the edge. I think it was your home-made raspberry jelly that made the difference.

As requested, I enclose the recipe I always use to make Semolina Cake. I hope it works out as well for you as it usually does for me.

Very best wishes, and I hope to meet you again sometime. If you are in the neighbourhood please pop in anytime, you'll be most welcome.

Yours sincerely

Ella Forbes Cowan

Semolina Cake

2 oz semolina

2 oz butter

2 oz sugar

1 egg (reconstituted)

1 tsp almond essence

Shortcrust pastry:
   4 oz plain flour and a pinch salt
   2 oz butter
   4 ttsps cold water (approx)

Jam or jelly

Line tin (a sandwich or patty tin) with shortcrust pastry. Spread with jam or jelly. Cream butter and sugar, add semolina and egg then essence. Place on top of jam or jelly and bake for 20 minutes in a moderate oven (turn up oven to hot for one minute to set pastry).

PAVLOVA

6 Egg Whites
12 ozs. Castor Sugar
2 teaspoons White Vinegar
2 level teaspoons cornflour
1 teaspoon vanilla essence.

(Egg Whites should be at room temp.)

Beat Egg Whites till stiff add castor
sugar very slowly just sprinkling it
into the mixture, and beat till mixture
is very stiff and will stand in peaks.
Add vinegar, cornflour and essence
and mix this in with a metal spoon.
Pour mixture onto a scone tray upside
down which has been lightly brushed
with melted butter.   Smooth into a
round but leaving it quite high about
2" or so.   Put on middle shelf of
oven pre-heated to 350° and bake for
20 minutes.   Reduce heat to 250°
and bake for further 1 hour.

Leave for a little while on tray then
turn upside down onto large serving plate
When cold top with ½ pint of Whipped
Cream and any topping pf choice.

Toppings which are suitable:

    Strawberries
    Chinese Goosberries
    Chocolate Peppermint Crisp
    Chocolate flake
    Pineapple
    Passionfruit

PEOPLE'S FRIEND
BAKING BOOK

Presented with 'PEOPLE'S FRIEND'

But an' Ben Clootie Dumpling

Ah'm no repeatin' mysel, this is a different recipe fae the twa dumplins in Maw Broon's Cookbook. I got it fae Eileen Smith. It's affy fine!

6 oz SR flour

6 oz brown breadcrumbs

6 oz suet

1 teaspoon bicarb o' soda

2 teaspoon cinnamon

2 teaspoon ginger

4 oz currants

6 oz sultanas

4 oz soft dark brown sugar

2 tablespoon syrup

Approx 1 1/2 cups milk

Place your cloot in boiling water. Mix all the ingredients together wi' the milk tae mak' a fairly soft consistency. Mak' sure it is weel mixed. Tak' the cloot oot o' the water an' wring, then lay flat oot an' dredge weel wi' flour. Smooth the flour over wi' your hands tae get an even spread. Place the mix on the cloot, leave room for expansion, tie wi' string. Simmer for 2-3 hours in large pan.

Tak oot o' pot, put in a colander untie string, place plate over an' turn oot. No need tae dry aff. Serve hot wi' syrup or cold wi' a cuppa!

127

Afore a Long Day Oot ...

In other words, hearty breakfasts an' brunches tae keep my family going on a busy or active day.

129

Banana Bread

If I buy bananas and they look like they are starting to turn, it is the perfect excuse to make this lovely banana bread. You need a 9-inch loaf tin.

2 eggs, beaten

80 ml buttermilk

120 ml vegetable oil

225 g mashed bananas

300 g sugar

220 g plain flour

1 teaspoon baking soda

$\frac{1}{2}$ teaspoon salt

Preheat oven to 165 degrees C. Butter the loaf tin. Mix together the liquids and bananas. Gradually add the liquid to the dry ingredients and mix well. Pour into loaf tin and bake for 1 hour 20 mins. Test with a skewer. If it comes out clean it's ready.

Spanish Hot Chocolate

2 cups full cream milk
4 oz 70%-cocoa chocolate
$\frac{1}{2}$ teaspoon instant coffee
Pinch ground nutmeg

Add all ingredients to a saucepan over a low heat.

Once the chocolate has melted the heat can be turned up because the milk needs to reach boiling point so it can be frothed. Remove from heat and whisk it strongly till frothy. Heat again and then whisk again. It should be frothier this time. Pour into two mugs.

2

Honey Cake

Highland Pa

21

RECIPE CARDS

250 g (8 oz) plain flour
1 tsp cinnamon
$\frac{1}{2}$ tsp mixed spice
$\frac{1}{2}$ tsp bicarbonate of soda
125 g (4 oz) butter
125 g (4 oz) brown sugar
1 egg, separated
125g (4 oz) honey
milk to mix
a little caster sugar

Preheat the oven to gas mark 4, 175°C, 350°F. Sieve the flour, spices and bicarbonate together. Cream the butter and brown sugar and beat in the egg yolk. Add the honey to this mixture. Fold in the dry ingredients gradually and gently, adding milk if the mixture is too thick. Whisk the egg white until stiff and fold gently into the mixture.

Grease or line a loaf tin and pour in the mixture evenly. Sprinkle the top with a little caster sugar so that the cake has a slightly crunchy surface.

Bake for approximately 30 minutes and test with a skewer. Dredge with more caster sugar when baked.

Wheaten Loaf

There's nae yeast in this, just baking soda, so there's nae need to let it rise, ye can bake it right away.

3 cups wheat flour
2 cups white flour
2 cups buttermilk
1 tablespoon syrup
1 teaspoon cream o' tartar
1 teaspoon baking soda
1/2 teaspoon salt

Dissolve the syrup in the milk, an' then combine wi' the dry ingredients tae mak' a soft dough. Put into a greased loaf tin, an' bake in a moderate oven for forty minutes. Turn oot onto a cake rack tae cool. Eat the next day — or if ye canna wait at least wait till it is cool — an' spread thick slices wi' butter.

Rolls
(quickly made without yeast)

1/2 lb. flour
One heaped teaspoonful baking powder
Half a teaspoonful salt
One tablespoonful lard or butter
About half a pint skimmed milk

Combine flour and fat as you do morning rolls. Cut out rounds with a large scone cutter, wet on one side. Bake at 425°F for about 20 minutes.

Crescent Rolls

Roll bread dough into a long thin strip about six inches wide; cut in triangles, wet the edges, and roll up, beginning with the base edge, rolling to the triangle's tip.

Make into the shape of a horseshoe.

Brush with melted butter, and bake in a quick oven.

Morning Rolls

Ye can mah' the dough for these the night afore, but it's best tae chill it so the yeast rises much mair slowly.

- 1lb strong plain flour
- 2 teaspoons salt
- 2 oz butter
- 1/2 oz dried yeast
- 1 tsp sugar
- 1/4 pint milk
- 1/4 pint tepid water

Rub fat, salt an' flour together wi' the fingertips. Warm the milk an' add the yeast an' sugar. Add tae the flour an' fat an' knead tae a soft dough for no less than ten minutes. The dough should be elastic. Place in an oiled bowl in a warm place an' cover wi' a damp tea towel for an hour. Turn dough oot o' bowl. Knock it back an' knead lightly. Divide into 6 or 7 rolls, put on a greased baking tray, cover an' leave tae prove for 30 minutes, they should roughly double in size. Brush wi' milk an' dust wi' flour an' bake at 425 °F for 15 tae 20 minutes.

Kippers

Kippers are braw for breakfast. Now, the But an' Ben is a bit wee to be cookin' kippers. The smell lingers on everything. So I like to cook them ootside in the big frying pan, wi' loads o' butter over a wee fire. The toast tastes best when it's made on a wee stick over the fire anyway. Spread toast thick wi' butter.

Fried Sheep's Kidneys

Never mind cereal, this is a real man's breakfast! *Ye can cook them yersel then!*

Skin the kidneys, wash them well in water.

Cut the kidneys in half lengthways.

Fry them in butter and serve them on hot buttered toast wi' grilled bacon and tomatoes.

Drop Scones

These are a tea-time treat really, but occasionally we hae them in the morning, though only at the But an' Ben. Joe likes them fried wi' his fry up!

Aye, they are braw to soak up your egg yolks and the juice o' yer fried tomatoes

2 tablespoons caster sugar
1 egg
1 tablespoon melted butter
1 cup buttermilk
2 cups plain flour
1 teaspoon baking soda
1 teaspoon cream o' tartar

Add the sugar tae the egg an' beat weel, then add the melted butter an' the milk. Put the dry ingredients in a bowl then add the liquid an' mix tae a thick batter. Heat the girdle till it is hot, an' grease it weel

Drap a wee spoonful o' batter onto the girdle. When ye see bubbles forming in the pancake's surface, turn it ower. As ye cook them, keep them wrapped in a clean tea towel till ye need them.

Spanish Eggs

On a guid year I can grow sweet peppers an' tomatoes in my wee glass frame in my gairden. This is a braw brunch dish served wi' a thick doorstep o' breid. Adding the wild garlic is awfy fine but it is only at its best in early summer. You can use bought spring onions and garlic instead though. Add half a seeded, chopped red chilli if you like it hot. I dinna like that but I can grow them in the greenhoose tae!

1 onion, chopped
1 red or green pepper, chopped
Oil or butter
Fower eggs, beaten
Twa firm peeled tomatoes, deseeded and chopped
Chopped stems o' wild garlic
Plenty salt and black pepper

see page 17 for how to peel tomatoes

Cook the pepper and onion till tender in oil or butter. Add the chopped tomatoes and garlic stems and mix well. Season to taste.

Add the eggs and stir till the mixture is soft and creamy. Enough for me and my laddie for brunch afore we go a big walk. It is awfy, awfy fine wi' a wee bit crispy bacon and some fried bread. My mooth's fair waterin' at the thought.

Boiled Eggs

I mentioned hard-boiled eggs earlier on (pages 11 and 20) — but I never mentioned runny boiled eggs. My boys (Paw an' Granpaw included) like runny-yolkit eggs, wi' wee toastie sodjers tae douk in them (God love them!). Farmer Wilson's hens quite often have double yolks an' they are a deep, dark orange — no' like they peely-wally yellow anes ye get wi' shop-bought eggs.

ALWAYS → WARN 9S!!

Lay eggs gently (in case o' cracking) into a pan o' cauld water, bring them tae the boil, an' use a timer at first sign o' the boil. Simmer efter it reaches boiling point:

—Runny yolks an' slightly runny white: simmer for 3 minutes.
—Runny yolk wi' white just set: simmer for 4 minutes.
—Soft but set yolk an' set white: simmer for 5 minutes.
—Hard boiled wi' slightly moist yolk: simmer for 6 minutes.
—Completely hard boiled: simmer for 7 minutes.

Bacon and Eggs

About fower guid thick slices o' Ayrshire bacon, fried, or grilled, till the fat is crispy, wi' twa sunny fried eggs and twa slices of buttered hame-made wheaten loaf is enough to keep me going for hours of walking. Hen is mair greedy than me and has sausages tae.

An' fried breid! An' toast an' jam. You need plenty o' carbs for energy ye ken!

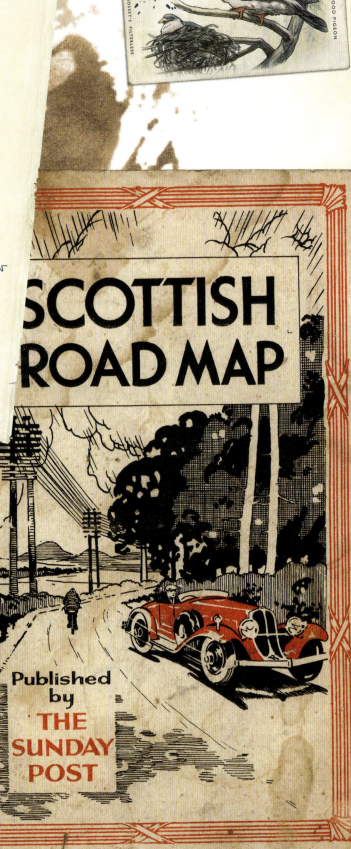

Poached Eggs

The lassies like their eggs poached, it's mair slimming than fried. Very fresh eggs poach the best, the white is thicker an' stays thegither better. Use a large wide pan o' boiling water, turn it doon tae simmer. Break the eggs carefully into the water, taking care no' tae mix the yolk an' white. Cook awfy gently till set, an' lift oot wi' a slotted spoon, drain aff all water an' serve on buttered toast.

For a lunch dish, dish up on a bed o' spinach, or green cabbage. Now that is awfy braw indeed.

Paw's Tip:
To stop ye gettin' car sick, haud a ten bob note between yer teeth.

141

Efter a Long Day Oot ...

Slow-cooked, quick-cooked an' store-cupboard comfort food tae eat efter a long day oot.

Fun can be hard work!

A Hay Box for Slow Cookin'

Maw got a slow cooker two Christmasses ago but this was what we did in the auld days. It saves you loads of money and electricity.

Find a wooden box with a good-fitting lid. Line the box all round with about 10 layers o' newspaper. Mak sure that the joins come in different places.

Nail a covering o' felt or flannel over the paper. Line the lid wi' felt tae.

You could attach the lid to the box wi' hinges. Mak sure you can fasten the lid down tightly. Fasten it shut with a hasp or tie it down.

Fill the box to the depth o' six inches wi' very tightly packed hay. Put the pots that you are going to use into the hay. Pack the hay tightly roon them so that when the pots are lifted oot their shape is left in the hay.

A cast-iron casserole dish is best for hay box use, as it keeps the heat well, and disna tak' up much room.

Firmly stuff a pillowcase wi' hay, and shape it so it fits exactly into the space between the top o' the pan and the lid o' the box.

Cook food for aboot 30 mins afore puttin' it in the hay box and mak sure it reaches the boil so that the heat reaches the middle o' even big bits o' meat.

Slow Cookin' in the Hay Box

Great if ye'll be oot a' day an' want your dinner tae be ready when ye come hame.

The food put in it needs a bit o' cookin' afore it is pit in the box, an' ye'll mebbe hae tae reheat it when it is taken oot, but it can be left for hours, an' ye dinna hae tae worry that it micht boil ower or burn.

The dish should be nearly full, tae keep the heat, but tak' care ye dinna spill ony juice amang the hay.

Food tahs fower times as long tae cook in a hay box as it does on the stove, an' dinna worry if it's left a lot longer.

Stews

Cook for half an hour on the stove, then finish aff in the hay box for four tae five hours, or it may be left all night.

Rice pudding

Ten minutes vigorous boiling, an' four tae five hours in the box.

Tatties

Boil for five minutes, cook in the box for twa tae three hours.

Chicken

About 30 minutes on the stove, an' 7 hours or all night in the box.

145

Beans and Bacon Casserole

One pint haricot beans
Four rashers o' bacon
One chopped onion
One teaspoonful golden syrup
One tablespoonful tomato sauce
Pepper, and salt if required

Soak the beans for twelve hours, cook them with a little water in a casserole till soft but not mushy.

Fry the bacon and onion, add them, the sauce, and syrup to the beans, make thoroughly hot in the oven, and serve in the casserole.

The beans may be entirely prepared the day before.

Rainy, rainy rattle-stanes
Dinna rain on me;
But rain on Johnnie
Groat's Hoose,
Far ower the sea.

Grilled Lamb Chops

Loin chops, about one inch or more in thickness: season with salt and pepper; place a little butter or fat on each; put under the grill for 4 or 5 minutes each side. If required well done with crispy fat, pierce fat, sprinkle it with salt and cook a long time at a low temperature.

Rabbit Casserole wi' Mustard

This can be cooked in the hay box too. Farmer Wilson gets me the rabbits (Paw an' Granpaw's hunting days are ower, thankfully!). Usual cooking time is 3 hrs 30 mins, so at least double that for cooking in the box. Use a cast iron casserole ye can use on the stove an' in the oven.

4 tbsp butter
2 rabbits, jointed
4 rashers fat bacon
10 oz onions, chopped
10 oz carrots, chopped
4 celery sticks, chopped
1 pint beer
2 teaaspoons mustard
2 bay leaves
2 garlic cloves, crushed

Brown the rabbit meat in butter. Tak' oot o' the pan. Fry bacon till crispy, add onions, carrots an' celery. Add beer an' reduce a little. Add mustard, bay leaves an' garlic, an' return rabbit tae pot. Cover an' cook in a moderate oven for about 3 hours.

147

Baked Mushrooms

½ lb mushrooms
One rasher of bacon, finely chopped
Pinches of nutmeg, pepper, salt
3 well-beaten eggs

Butter
Breadcrumbs

Clean the mushrooms. Remove the stalks but dinna waste them, put them in a pan of salted water to boil for stock for another dish.

Chop up six mushrooms, cook in the pan with the chopped bacon and the seasonings and cook till bacon fat is crispy.

Add the eggs, and stir over gentle heat till creamy but not cooked. Fill the gill side of the rest of the mushrooms with this mixture, sprinkle with breadcrumbs and bits of butter.

Lay the filled mushrooms on a greased oven dish, and brown in a hot oven.

THAT WHICH SHOULD ACCOMPANY OLD AGE: HONOUR, LOVE, OBEDIENCE, TROOPS OF FRIENDS.

Curry

Now this is no' authentic — this is an auld-fashioned version o' curry that my Mammy used tae mak' tae use up leftovers.

2 onions, finely chopped
1 clove o' garlic, chopped (my mither never used the garlic but I like it)
1 oz butter
1 heaped tablespoon curry powder
1/2 tablespoon curry paste
1 pint chicken stock
A grated aipple
A handful o' raisins
About 4oz leftover meat per person, cooked or raw

Fry the onion an' garlic in the butter, add the powder, an' paste an' fry for a further twa minutes wi' the meat if meat is raw.

Stir in the liquid, bring tae the boil, add cooked meat, aipple an' raisins, an' gently simmer. If the meat is raw, stew slowly till tender; if previously cooked, reheat thoroughly.

Martha's Beef Goulash

2 lbs stewing steak, cubed
Seasoned flour (wi' white pepper, salt, an'
  paprika) *I tried this wi' smoked paprika — much nicer!*
1 tablespoon o' beef dripping
1 onion, chopped
1 stalk celery, chopped
1 pint beef stock
1 tablespoon tomato purée
1 tin chopped tomatoes
1 clove
3 potatoes, peeled an' cubed
Parsley, chopped

Toss the meat in seasoned flour. Melt the dripping in a cast iron casserole an' brown the meat in it. Tak' oot the meat. Add the onions an' celery an' sweat till soft.

Return the meat tae the pan. Add the stock, tomato purée an' the clove. Cover pan tightly, an' simmer gently till the meat is tender (aboot 2 hours).

Then add the potato. Continue cooking till potato is soft. Add the chopped parsley an' dish up. Or ye can mah' it the night afore an' reheat — it tastes even better the next day. Again, I mah' twa batches for my lot!

Egg Pie

/ This pie can be made the night afore and it disna tak' that long tae heat up when ye get in efter a long day oot walking. Guid for using up leftover tatties, not that there are many leftovers when my family are aboot.

4 hard-boiled eggs
1/2 pint o' white sauce see page 98
3 cups cooked potatoes
Seasoning to taste

Hard boil the eggs an' chop them. Mash the cooked potatoes. Make white sauce. Mix the eggs in the sauce, and fill a greased oven dish with alternate layers o' the egg mixture and potato. Finish with potato. Rough over the top with a fork. Brush with melted butter, and sprinkle salt and pepper on top. Chill till ready to eat and reheat in moderate oven for about 45 minutes (watch for it bubbling).

Egg and Ham Pie

Grease a pie tin, line it with short-crust pastry. Fill it with alternate layers o' uncooked ham and chopped boiled egg. Cover with pastry, and bake in at 375°F for aboot 25 minutes.

Vegetable Pie

This pie can be made the night afore.

2 ozs butter
1 wee carrot
1 cup garden peas
1 large onion
2 or 3 stalks celery
3 skinned tomatoes
2 cups white sauce (mind, I telt ye how
   tae mak' it on page 98)

Melt the butter, chop the onion, carrot,
an' celery, fry them slowly till soft.
   Add the rest o' the ingredients, add the
white sauce, pour into the pie dish, cover
wi' short-crust pastry or mashed potato
crust. Bake for three quarters o' an hour
in a moderate oven.

Potato Crust:
Mash 1/2 lb potatoes while still warm,
add a dod o' butter an' a spoon o' beaten
egg. You'll mebbe need tae add a spoonful
o' flour tae mak' it firm enough tae
roll. Roll oot about half an inch thick,
an' cover the pie. Brush ower the top wi'
melted butter.

Vegetable Bake

This can, for the maist part, be made the night afore except for whipping the eggs. It's quite easy tae prepare efter a long day though.

2 cups cauliflower
2 cups broccoli (or any veg ye prefer)
2 oz butter
2 cups brown breadcrumbs
1 cup milk
1 onion, chopped
2 eggs, yolks an' whites separated
Pepper, salt, an' a bit o' nutmeg

add a few chopped fried mushrooms too

Fry the onions in half the butter. Boil the ither vegetables but dinna ower cook. Drain, an' melt the rest o' the butter ower them. Soak the breadcrumbs in the milk till milk is sooked up. Mix the vegetables, onions an' beaten yolks wi' the breadcrumbs, an' season it. Whip the egg whites till stiff. Fold them into the vegetable mixture.

Pour the mixture into a greased oven dish wi' a lid, cover an' bake in a moderate oven for aboot 40 minutes. A few minutes afore the end, tak the cover aff, put grated cheese, sliced tomatoes an' black pepper on top and cook for aboot ten minutes mair till cheese melts. Spoon it oot the tin. Serves about fower hungry folk wi' baked tatties an' cold meat.

155

Baked Eggs

I'm no' a great one for cooking, but while Maw gets the bairns ready for their beds I can get this easy supper dish ready while they tell each other stories or talk about the things they got up to that day.

Butter ramekin dishes, and dust with pepper and salt. Break in the egg carefully, dust again with pepper and salt, and put a dod of butter on the top. Bake in a moderate oven for about 15 minutes or till the eggs are as firm as you need. Have this with toast soldiers and butter (we can make the toast on forks by the fire too — the bairns think it tastes better that way).

Toast an' Mushrooms

There's no really a recipe tae this recipe, but me an' Granpaw like it for oor supper. My one tip is to put nutmeg on the mushrooms.

Fower thick doorsteps o' broon breid
Butter
As many dark, open, field mushrooms as we can get oor hands on, for politeness sake let's say half a pound.

Fry mushrooms. Toast breid. Butter breid. Put mushrooms on it. Eat. Braw!

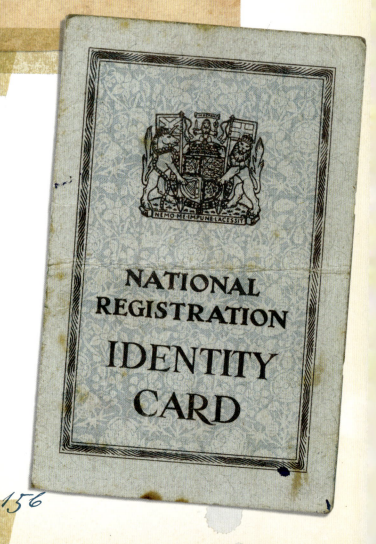

Mince

Mince an' tatties — the best comfort food known tae man ... or wummin!

I believe makin' guid mince is an art, an' I won't hear otherwise. Farmer Wilson's lean steak mince is the best roon these pairts.

Brown it thoroughly in its ain fat — browning creates flavour. Then add some guid-sized chopped sweet onions an' slowly fry alang wi' the browned mince. Then add gravy an' chopped carrots. The gravy should be made fae guid stock an' thickened wi' a teaspoon o' cornflour. Then cook it slow — if mince boils the meat gets hard. For a one-pot meal add sliced tatties straight tae the cooking pot* see below an' simmer covered for about 20 minutes.

Mince can be made the night afore an' heated up when ye get hame frae a long day oot. Awfy fine!

We know -> that, we've seen some o' your boyfriends, Daph

* I prefer doughballs
1 rounded tbsp SR flour and 1 level tbsp suet per person
Season the flour and suet (add chopped herbs if ye like). Mix tae a stiff dough wi' water. Put spoonfuls o' dough on top o' the mince. Put the lid back on and cook 20 mins.

157

Sardine Toast

A quick tasty supper straight fae the storecupboard. To be eaten while Paw tells ghost stories by the fire!

Tinned sardines
Lemon
Hot toast
Butter

Drain the oil fae the fish, rub off any skin and remove bones. Mash with a fork till smooth and season with salt and pepper and a wee squeeze o' lemon. Spread on hot buttered toast, wi' chopped tomatoes tae.

Hen's Mixed Grill

Ah'm no' much o' a cook but I can manage this f... me an' Joe when we stay here by oorsels.

2 lamb chops (each)
2 pork sausages (each)
2 or 3 big mushrooms (each)
2 rashers o' bacon (each)
2 tomatoes, halved (each)
Pepper and salt (each ... oops ... got confused there)

I like my lamb chops well done, wi' crispy fat, so I grill them first, slowly, under a low heat for a long time. Joe likes his wi' the fat cut aff and cooked medium, so when mine is done I put it to the side, turn up the heat, put his on at the same time as the sausage and bacon. Dinna pierce the sausages. Tak' the big mushrooms and put a dod o' butter and a shake o' salt on the gills of each one and pop them gill-side up, under the grill. Grill the tomatoes tae, wi' a wee shake o' pepper on each ane. As things cook, put them to one side to keep warm. Serve very h... ... wi' some sort o' vegetable. Cabbage and butter is guid wi' it.

Welsh Rarebit

250 g (8 oz) mature cheddar cheese, grated
3 tbsp milk
6 g (^{1}/4 oz) flour
25 g (1 oz) butter
^{1}/2 tsp mustard
3 thsps real ale (optional)
1 tsp Worcestershire sauce
1 egg yolk
4 slices of thick toasted bread, crusts
   removed
salt and pepper

Melt the cheese in the milk in a saucepan over a moderate heat without boiling. Add the mustard, Worcestershire sauce, flour and butter and stir. Beat up the egg yolk and mix with the real ale.

Remove the sauce from the heat and mix in the egg yolk mixture. Place the toast in a heatproof dish and cover with the cheese sauce.

Brown under the grill and serve at once. Serves two to four.

Welsh ~~Rabbit~~ Rarebit

The only rabbit The Bairn will eat.

1 teaspoon cornflour
4 tablespoons milk
2 teaspoons butter
6 ozs grated cheese
1 teaspoon mustard
Pepper an' salt

Mak' twa slices o' thick toast. Blend the cornflour wi' the milk. Melt the butter in a saucepan, an' add the cornflour, milk, cheese, an' seasonings. Heat gently and stir till smooth an' creamy.

Pour onto the toast an' dish up immediately.

Daphne's Special Chilli

Everyone's chilli has a secret ingredient, mine's is prunes. I like HOT chilli and the sweetness o' the prunes adds a bit extra flavour and counteracts some of the bitterness in the spices (ye canna tell that it's prunes in there, by the way). This can also be bunged in the slow cooker as long as you brown the mince first and fry the onions, or it can be made the day afore. It always tastes better the second day.

1 kg lean steak mince
2 large onions, chopped
1 carrot, diced
2 sticks celery, finely chopped
Splash o' red wine
5 cloves garlic, crushed or finely chopped
2 teaspoons smoked parika
2 teaspoons chilli powder
$1/2$ teaspoon celery salt
$1/2$ teaspoon white pepper
$1/2$ teaspoon dried oregano
2 teaspoons cumin
2 sweet red peppers, diced
1 chilli pepper, deseeded and finely chopped
2 tins chopped tomatoes
1 tin kidney beans
Around 1 pint beef stock
6 soft prunes, finely chopped

I hate it when Daphne makes chilli at the But an' Ben. It aye tastes guid, but it makes the whole place stink o' garlic.

Ye'll no' be wanting ony next time then, Paw. Cheek!

In a large frying pan or wok thoroughly brown the mince in its ain fat. Add the spices. Add the onions and celery and cook till soft. Add the wine and reduce. Add the garlic and peppers and chilli. Add the tinned tomatoes and the stock, the prunes and simmer for about 30 minutes. Taste. Add more stock if you think it is a bit dry. Serve with basmati rice and with sour cream on top. Serves 6.

Lamb Hot Pot

2 lb o' lean chopped lamb

2 lbs potatoes, peeled, parboiled an' sliced

1 lb o' onions, chopped an' sweated in
  2 ozs butter

4 carrots, peeled an' cut in circles

3 sheep's kidneys

1/2 lb mushrooms, cleaned an' chopped

1/2 pint lamb stock

Pepper, salt

Mak' sure the lamb is chopped in even-sized pieces. Remove as much fat as possible. Wash, skin an' slice the kidneys. Brown the lamb. Parboil the tatties, then slice. Arrange all o' the separate ingredients in layers in a casserole wi' a guid-fittin' lid. Sprinkle each layer wi' seasoning. The sliced tatties are tae go on top. Pour lamb stock ower it. Put some wee dods o' butter on the tatties. Cover wi' the lid, an' cook for aboot three hours in a slow oven. Tak' the lid aff, turn the oven up, an' leave the casserole in tae brown. Ye can dish up immediately or it can be reheated.

Cinnamon Apples

4 large, tart apples, cores removed,
  unpeeled
1/4 cup brown sugar
1 tsp cinnamon
1/4 cup chopped sultanas, soaked in
  apple juice
1 or 2 cups cider
1 tbsp butter

Soak sultanas in cider overnight. Drain
but keep liquid. Chop sultanas up,
mix wi' sugar and cinnamon. Stuff the
hollowed-out apples wi' this. Bring
one cup cider to the boil. Pour over
the apple. Put a dod o' butter on each
apple. Bake in a slow oven for 30 tae
40 minutes.

Custard

2 tsps cornflour
4 egg yolks
1 oz sugar
1 pint full cream milk
1 tsp vanilla essence

Blend the cornflour with
a little cold milk.
Heat the remainder of
the milk. Pour in the
blended cornflour. Whisk
with balloon whisk
till boiling and cook
thoroughly. Beat yolks an
sugar together in a bowl.
When cool enough, pour the
thickened milk mixture
over the eggs in the bowl
and whisk. Return to
the pan and whisk over
the heat until the egg is
cooked, but don't boil!
Add vanilla. Serve hot or
cold.

Mock Cream

1/2 can milk (Evap.)
1 tablesp. sugar
1   "   gelatine
1   "   boiling water
vanilla essence

Empty milk into basin add sugar
& essence dissolve gelatine in
boiling water mix well + beat
till stiff

Sultana Tarts

Ye can mak these beforehand an' just reheat an' eat wi' cream or custard. It'll mak' aboot a dozen wee tarts.

2 oz butter
2 oz sugar
1 egg, beaten weel
4 oz sultanas
½ cup apple or grape juice
½ cup water
1 oz mixed peel
A grated apple
A packet o' shortcrust pastry

Soak the sultanas in the half cup of juice and half cup of water overnight. Strain. Melt the butter. Mix a' the ingredients thegither weel, except any leftover juice and water from the soaking sultanas, discard that.

Cut pastry into 24 circles. Line your tart tins wi' 12 pastry circles. Fill wi' fruit filling. Top wi' pastry circles an' seal, leaving a hole in top o' each.

Bake at 350 °F for about 20 minutes.

Holiday Feasts at the But an' Ben

Holidays are great fun at the But an' Ben — we hae some smashing memories o' guid times spent thegither ... maistly involving eating! Whatever the time o' year, whatever the weather, the best times are when we are a' here.

Holiday feasts mean things that are a bit mair work. They mean roasts an' game (in season or saved for a special occasion oot the freezer), an' mair expensive (an' fattening!) food that we widnae hae every day.

Granmaw's recipe

Roast Venison with Herb Crumb Topping

Make a breadcrumb an' herb coating for the meat. Venison can be dry — this helps keep the moisture in. Take ony raw juices fae the meat an' mix wi' some breadcrumbs, melted butter, salt, an' some chopped fresh thyme.

Put on top o' the meat an' cover in foil. Roast 20 minutes per lb at 350°F. Then during the last 15 mins tak' the foil aff so you can crisp the crumbs up.

Mak' sauce for it wi' beef stock, ony roasting juices, red wine, flour, sugar, cinnamon, an' butter an' salt.

Painting Boiled Eggs for Easter

What you need:

1/2 cup water
Approx 30 drops (or **more**) food colouring
1 tsp vinegar
Boiled eggs

Method:

Boil the water. Drop in the food colouring of your choice. Add the vinegar and allow it to cool. Dip a boiled egg into the dye (use an old slotted spoon for this) and leave to steep until you can see it has achieved the colour you want.

Spoon it **out and pat dry** with tissues.

Let it **sit** for 30 minutes to dry. You could sit it in a cardboard egg container **for this.** This can be a base coat on top of which you could draw or paint other patterns.

Or why not tie some string or rubber **bands** around the egg before dipping in the **dye** to get a **stripey** effect.

You can wrap a strip of sticky **tape** around the egg before dyeing to make bigger **stripes**. Drop candle wax on the **egg** before dyeing to **make** spots.

hen's egg

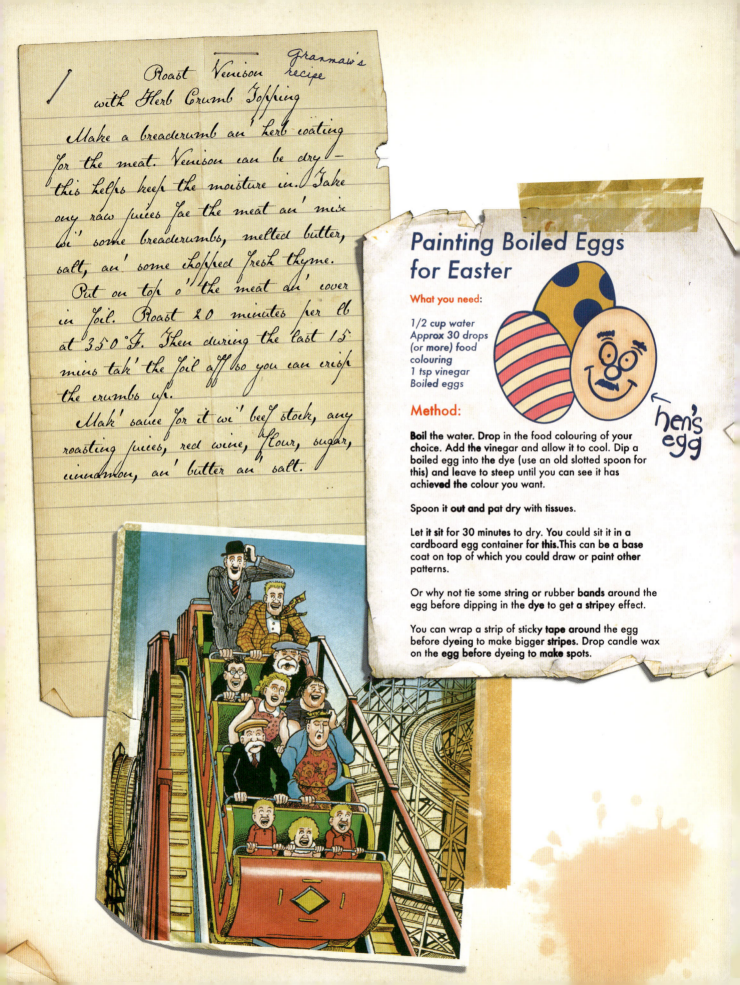

Shrove Tuesday Pancakes

These are no' jist for Shrove Tuesday. We hae them for breakfast on Easter Sunday afore we go oot an' roll oor eggs. I mak' the batter the night afore. It is meant tae improve it, but it is jist handy having it made up for the next day.

4 oz. flour
1/2 pint milk
2 eggs
Pinch o' salt

Sieve the flour an' salt into a bowl, add the eggs an' as much o' the milk as will mak' a fairly thick batter.

Beat this wi' a whisk till the surface is covered wi' bubbles, add the rest o' the milk, an' allow it tae stand.

Pour the batter into a jug that has a spout.

Coat a small non-stick frying pan wi' butter, an' when it is smoking hot, pour in a thin layer o' the batter, an' cook first one side, then the other.

Serve wi' lemon an' sugar, or jam or syrup, or stewed apple.

SIMNEL CAKE

I'll to thee a Simnell bring
'Gainst thou go'st a mothering,
So that, when she blesseth thee,
Half that blessing thou'lt give to me.
                        Robert Herrick 1648

¹/₂ lb butter,
¹/₂ lb caster sugar
¹/₂ lb raisins
¹/₂ lb sultanas
¹/₂ lb currants
¹/₂ lb flour, sifted
4 ozs mixed candied peel, finely chopped
¹/₂ teaspoon each ground ginger and cinnamon
Good pinch nutmeg
5 well-beaten eggs
1 teaspoon baking powder

Grease a 9-inch cake tin and line it with grease-proof paper. Wrap thick paper around the tin and secure it with strong string; preheat the oven to 30°F.

Cream the butter and sugar, beat in each egg with a very little flour and beat for about ten minutes. Add the rest of the flour, the fruit, the spices, and the baking powder. Pour into the tin, and give the tin a sharp thump before baking for 2 hours.

If the top starts to get too brown too quickly, cover it with dampened kitchen roll.

Test with a heated skewer or knitting needle, and if it comes out clean take out the cake. Let it stand for a minute to let the steam escape, then turn onto a cake rack. When cold, level the cake if need be and cover with almond icing.

Almond Icing
6 ozs ground almonds
3 ozs icing sugar
3 ozs caster sugar
1 well-beaten egg
1 teaspoon vanilla essence
¹/₂ teaspoon orange flower water
Few drops almond essence

Pound the sugars and almond till well mixed, add the flavourings, and make into a stiff paste with the egg.

Dust the board with fine sugar, roll out the icing a size smaller than the top of the cake, lay it on, and press it to the size.

Make the sides level with the top, brush over with egg, score across the top with the back of the knife, and put under a hot grill for a minute or two to get the almond icing slightly brown.

For Maw on Mother's Day

Why We Have Hot Cross Buns, by Horace Broon

In the 13th century, Sister Clare, AKA Saint Clare, was the abbess of a convent near Assisi. Pope Innocent IV came to visit her (Maybe it was Easter and he went there to roll his eggs, anyway ...). At dinner she asked him to bless the bread. He told her to make the sign of the Cross over the loaves, and a cross is said to have appeared on each one. History does not tell whether they then spread them wi' butter and jeely and ate them or no'.

WhaT do YoU geT if YoU poUR hoT WaTeR doon a RabbiT hole?

HoT, cRoSS bUnnies

ach, that joke was doing the rounds when Granpaw was a boy.

GRanpaw WaS neVeR a boY!

Hot Cross Buns

1 oz fresh yeast

1/2 pint lukewarm milk

1 lb flour

1 teaspoon mixed spice

4 ozs caster sugar

4 ozs butter

1/2 teaspoon cinnamon

1 egg, weel beaten

2 oz sultanas

Some shortcrust pastry (recipe is in here somewhere) see page 120

Mix the yeast wi' the warm milk. Sieve the flour an' spice into a warmed bowl. Wi' your fingers, rub in the butter. Add the sugar, then the yeast an' milk, an' the egg. Knead into an elastic dough. Return tae the bowl, cover wi' a tea towel an' set in a warm place tae rise for twa hours. Knock back an' then knead in the sultanas. Form into buns, an' put them on a greased tin, brush ower wi' milk or egg, an' put a cross o' thin pastry on the top. Let them prove for a further 15 minutes. Then bake at aboot 375°F for aboot 20 minutes.

Gingerbread

1 lb self-raising flour

1 teaspoon mixed spice

2 teaspoons dried ginger

1 teaspoon cinnamon

4 ozs brown sugar

1 cup golden syrup

6 ozs butter

2 ozs crystallised ginger, finely chopped

4 ozs sultanas

2 eggs, separated

One cup buttermilk

Sieve the flour and spices into a bowl. Melt the butter and syrup. Separate the eggs. Beat the yolks with the sugar and add to the milk. Add the melted butter and syrup. Pour into the flour and mix well. Add the crystallised ginger and sultanas. Beat the egg whites till firm and fold into mixture.

Pour into a greased 12-inch Yorkshire tin and bake at 350°F for about three-quarters of an hour. Test with a skewer. Cool on a rack and cut into squares.

Hallow Fair
by Horace Broon

Hallow Fairs were held in Scotland on the first day of November. Few visitors to these fairs left without a gingerbread cake.

The mixture was once baked in all sorts of shapes — houses with gilded roofs, lions and tigers with gilded manes, kings and queens with golden crowns — hence the expression "the gilt is off the gingerbread."

Horace, I have never, ever heard anyone say "the gilt is off the gingerbread" ... However, I have heard someone say "Is that gingerbreid aff?"

I regularly say: "Go on, gies another bit o' gingerbreid. Oh, and how aboot a cup o' tea wi' three sugars tae?"

I admire the way you're no ashamed o' being greedy, Hen.

Roast Grouse

Grouse is in season fae 12th August till the beginning o' December. During shooting season the boys have helped oot as beaters an' have been given the odd grouse as pairt o' their payment.

I think they are best roasted (the grouse not the boys!) but tak' care tae keep them moist.

Rub them a' ower wi' butter or lard, cover the breast wi' thinly cut bacon an' roast in the oven, for 25 tae 30 minutes. Keep the natural juices o' the bird for gravy.

Ye can cook the bird's liver as an accompaniment. Fry for ten minutes, then mash wi' butter, an' spread on toast. Or ye can put it inside the bird mixed wi' a dod o' butter an' a squeeze o' lemon juice.

Serve wi' skirlie, game chips, cumberland sauce, tatties an' green vegetables.

Auld Alliance Pudding

This serves 6 … so I hae tae mak twa trays an' then the boys fight ower the spare yin!

5 oz finely grated
 orange rind

4 fl oz orange juice

2 fl oz Cointreau

1 tsp bicarbonate o' soda

2 ¼ oz butter,

2 ¼ oz caster sugar

2 eggs, beaten

15 oz self-raising flour

The sauce

7oz butter

14 oz brown sugar

2 tbsp Cointreau or
 orange liqueur

double cream

Preheat the oven tae 370°F. Mix the rind, bicarbonate o' soda an' the juice an' liqueur together in a bowl. Cream the butter an' sugar. In alternate spoonfuls add the eggs an' the flour, an' then mix rind mixture in. Pour into a greased 8-inch square cake tin. Bake for 35 tae 40 minutes.

Mak' the sauce. Melt the butter in a pan. Add the sugar, Cointreau an' cream, simmer an' stir till it starts tae thicken. Cut sponge into squares an' serve wi' sauce poured ower an' wi' whipped fresh cream.

173

Tin size $7\frac{1}{2} \times 5\frac{1}{2} \times 3$

Gingerbread. (ISA's)

1 cup milk	2 cups S.R. Flour
2 oz marg	1 teasp cinnamon
2 tablesp. treacle	1 " mixed spice
1 egg	$\frac{3}{4}$ cup sugar
~~pinch salt~~	$\frac{1}{2}$ teasp. baking soda
	pinch salt.

Melt marg. milk & treacle. Cool. Add beaten egg
350° middle shelf. $\frac{1}{2}$ hr.

Isa's scone.

5 tablesps. Flour
4 " milk   Melt marg. add to flour; with sugar
3 " sugar   milk & beaten egg
2 ozs. marg
1 egg   350° with gingerbread.

There's that missing bit o' jigsaw puzzle

Pity the rest of it is in the charity shop.

Sauce For Duck

$\frac{3}{4}$ pint beef gravy

A glass of sherry

A pinch of sugar

The juice of a lemon

The juice and zest of an orange

Add all ingredients except zest and reduce to

about half a pint. Add zest, simmer.

Sieve. Reheat when required.

Rum Butter.

$\frac{3}{4}$ lb. brown sugar (sft)
$\frac{1}{2}$ lb Butter of marg.
1 Glass of Rum
melt butter (not too hot).
mix in the sugar stir well
add rum mix well in

Roast Duck

Ducks are in season fae August till January, ducklings fae May till August. They are darker in colour than chickens an' the flesh is richer an' strong-tasting.

Roast wi' an apple or an onion inside for moisture.

Allow about 20 minutes tae the pound in a moderate oven, basting every ten minutes. Ten minutes afore ye dish up, brush over wi' butter, honey an' salt, an' return tae the oven tae crisp the skin.

Duck is often served wi' orange sauce or wi' cherries. Ye can get a load o' gean berries in summer around the But an' Ben. Geans are wild cherries an' they mak a braw sauce 'cause they are that wee bit sharper than bought cherries.

Duck is nice wi' green beans an' steamed celery.

*That's yoor opinyin!
Celery is evil*

With pinking shears cut wee gift cards from this years Christmas Cards You'll never use them but you can feel frugal and creative at the same time Punch wee hole in corner ad thread thin christmas ribbon

Use a mild solution of bleach to wash white gloss paintwork. It won't streak or bloom so you won't have to buff up

Stuffing for a Goose

3 cups breadcrumbs
1 cooking apple, peeled, cored an' grated
¼ cup melted butter
½ cup currants
½ cup chopped raisins
Pepper, salt, and paprika.

Mix a' the ingredients weel.

THE PHEASANT

GROSSET'S FILTERLESS

Stuffing for Duck or Goose

1 cup dried apricots
Pepper, salt, and paprika
2 ½ cups breadcrumbs
4 tablespoons melted butter

Rinse the apricots, soak them overnight in water and cook till nearly tender. Drain and chop them. add the breadcrumbs and seasoning, and moisten with the melted butter. Stuff the bird with it or alternatively, bind mixture together with a beaten egg, roll in egg then breadcrumbs, wrap in foil and cook in a moderate oven for about 30 minutes.

Roast Goose

Goose is in season fae October tae February. It is a braw dish for Christmas or New Year an' ae year we had it on New Year's day instead o' steak pies. It wis a braw yin fae Farmer Gray.

Tak' a 12-lb goose an' wash it weel in cauld water. Dry it thoroughly, stuff it wi' yer chosen stuffing, an' truss it for roasting. I actually prefer tae cook the stuffing on its ain in the oven – wrapped in foil. Then I'm no' worrying that the bird is no' cooked richt through.

It is a fatty bird so there's nae need tae coat it in butter. Wrap in foil in a baking tin, breast side doon. Pour in some cider or aipple juice an' seal up the foil parcel. Allow 20 tae 25 minutes tae the pound in a moderate oven.

Things tae eat wi' it: A stuffing that's made o' dried apricots is nice wi' goose, an' I like a breid sauce wi' it.

Serve wi' roast tatties — done in the goose fat — oh! They're just braw! Chestnuts an' brussels sprouts are guid tae.

Two Stuffings

Lemon and Parsley

½ lb fresh breadcrumbs
2 oz butter
White pepper and salt
Some grated lemon zest
1 cup chopped parsley
2 onions, chopped and fried
1 well beaten egg to bind

Sage and Onion

½ lb fresh breadcrumbs
2 oz butter
White pepper and salt
10 finely chopped sage leaves
4 onions, choopped and fried
1 well beaten egg to bind

Mix the dry ingredients together, bind with egg. stuff in the bird's cavity and remember to adjust the cooking time. for this extraweight. or pour into a greased loaf tin. cover in foil and bake till firm

Bread Sauce

1 onion
1 pint milk
¼ lb. stale breadcrumbs
crushed black pepper and salt to taate

chop and fry the onion till soft. heat the milk in a saucepan, add the fried onions and seasonings and bring to nearly boiling point. Add the crumbs gradually, stirring all the time, and cook till thick and creamy. sieve or blend the mixture till smooth.

THE LONG-TAILED TIT

GROSS...

THE NIGHTINGALE

GROSSET'S FILTERLESS

Cherry cake.

12 oz. flour. ¼ teasp. salt
½ teasp. B.P. 4 - 6g. cherries.
9 oz. butter 9oz caster sugar
3 eggs. 4 if small.
Milk to mix if needed
Vanilla essence.
7½ x 3½ Sieve flour, salt and B.P. into bowl. chop cherries. and mix with flour cream butter + sugar until light + fluffy. Gradually beat in eggs one at a time. Stir in dry ingredients adding a little ~~at a time~~ milk if needed to make anthine dropping consist Add essence 350° for 1½ hrs.

Sultana bun.

12 oz Pl. flour
9 oz mixed fruit
9g Sugar
9oz marg.
¾ teasp. Baking Powder
4 eggs.

375 - 350 2 hrs.

cream marg + sugar
Add fruit + b. powder
Then add flour + eggs
a little at a time.

Roast Chicken

Farmer Gray aye picks me oot some guid birds — an' he sends them tae me at the But an' Ben already plucked, trussed an' ready for cooking. I get the giblets tae!

Then a' ye have tae dae is stuff it ... or sometimes I jist stick an onion inside it an' cook the stuffing separately wrapped in foil. Coat the birdie in butter an' sprinkle wi' salt an' pepper. Put slices o' bacon across it.

Roast, 20 minutes tae the pound, in a moderate oven. Baste regularly. In the last 20 minutes o' cooking tah' aff the bacon an' let the skin brown.

Lift oot, pour aff maist o' the fat, mah' the gravy, an' serve the chicken wi' bacon or wee sausages, an' bread sauce in a separate dish.

Granmaw Broon's Steak Pie

I need tae mak twa o' these for my lot!

2 lb stewing steak

1 tablespoon seasoned plain flour

2 oz dripping

1 large onion, chopped

3 large carrots

1 pint beef stock

Worcestershire sauce

9 oz puff pastry

Toss the steak in the seasoned flour. Melt the dripping in a saucepan an' brown the meat. Remove an' put aside. Fry onions an' carrots. Return the meat tae the pan. Add the beef stock an' a dash o' Worcestershire sauce, black pepper an' salt. Cover an' bring tae the boil, then reduce the heat an' simmer, covered, for twa hours, checking noo an' again. Pour the stew into a 3-pint ashet. Roll oot the pastry an' press doon firmly on top o' the stew an' around the sides o' the ashet. Brush the top wi' beaten egg or some milk, an' score into crisscrosses. Mak' a hole in the centre tae let the steam oot. Cook for 30 minutes in the centre o' a hot oven.

Ella Cowan's Black Bun

Cake mixture:

1 lb flour

1/2 teaspoon ground ginger

1 teaspoon cream of tartar

1 teaspoon baking soda

1 teaspoon spice

1/2 teaspoon black pepper

1/2 lb brown sugar

1 lb currants, soaked in brandy

1/2 lb raisins

2 oz mixed peel, chopped

2 oz chopped almonds

1 beaten egg, 2 tablespoons brandy

Some buttermilk for binding

Pastry to line the cake tin:

3/4 lb flour

4 ozs margarine

1/2 teaspoon baking powder

Cold water

Make the pastry. Roll it out thinly and line the tin. Trim, leaving an inch to fold over, and make sure there's enough left to make a round to top the cake. Mix the dry ingredients and fruit. Gradually mix in the egg, then brandy, then buttermilk to a dropping consistency. Pour it into the 8-inch tin on top of the pastry. Fold the edges of the pastry over. Make four holes in the cake with a skewer. Lay a round of pastry on top of the cake mixture. Prick the pastry lightly with a fork. Bake in a moderate oven for 4 hours..

...ead is often attributed to Ma ...t Tails" might simply be nam ...ng of the genteel Edinburgh ladi ...shortbread with their afterno ...tion of "petits gastels"; "gaste ...aux". It is said that Mary's coo ...hem from France to Holyroo ...but there was certainly a stro ...wo countries in the days of t ...of the "fancier" Scottish recip may have originated in France.

At one time, in some parts of Scotland, a cake ...shortbread was broken over the bride's head "for luck" ...she stepped over the threshold of her new home. It was s... that if it broke into small pieces then the marriage would ...fruitful.

At one time considered a luxury, shortbread was only ma... on special occasions such as Christmas and Hogmanay.

Formerly, of course, it would have been thought a cri... to make shortbread with anything but the best fresh butt... but times are changed since butter cost ...w pence a po...

if ye did that wi Daphne's shortbreid the bride wid get concussion →

182

Shortbread

8 ozs flour
8 ozs butter
4 ozs semolina
4 ozs castor sugar

Mix all the ingredients into a dough that looks something like shortcrust, divide in twa, an' press into rounds. (Dinna handle or roll it too much or ye'll toughen the dough.

Pinch the edges, prick the surface wi' a fork, lay the shortbread rounds on a greased baking sheet. Score wi' lines that will help ye tae break the biscuits later.

If only one round is being made from this dough, a band o' tin foil should be put round the edges tae stop it fae burning. (Smaller biscuits made from the dough will cook quicker.)

Put the round into a hot oven for a little tae "set", then reduce the heat an' bake till are light brown an' firm tae the touch. Cool aff on a wire rack.

Broons' Hogmanay Traditions

* The telly is no' allowed (there isnae ane at the But an' Ben onyway).
* Try to stop Maw fae getting into a cleaning frenzy and deciding to clean oot under the sink at 11.30pm on Hogmanay.
* Break oot Granpaw's various home brews.
* Joe plays the pipes and the accordion and we have a sing song ... though the But an' Ben is too wee to do Strip the Willow.
* A'body has to do a turn! And even if it is rubbish (... please don't let Paw recite Tam O' Shanter again this year ...) everyone must cheer.

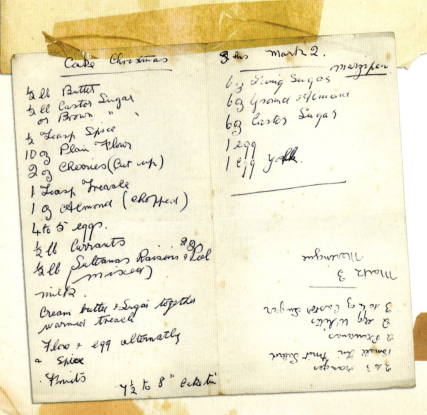

Hogmanay Traditions

Prepare your house and make it clean for visitors.

Have Black Bun and shortbread ready to give your guests and have a steak pie ready for the next day.

Kiss and shake hands with your loved ones (and, indeed, complete strangers) on the stroke of midnight.

Prepare to welcome dark-haired men into your home!

"First Foots" – the first person to cross the threshold of your home in the New Year must bear gifts, usually shortbread, or a cake, or a wee dram , and a lump of coal!

It is meant to be unlucky for the first foot to be a red or fair-haired man, or a woman.

The singing of Robert Burns' "Auld Lang Syne" is now a worldwide tradition.

Baked Ham

This is much mair tasty than boiled ham, but no' quite so thrifty 'cause it is dearer tae cook in the oven and when I boil it I aye use the cooking water for the stock for my lentil soup. (Ham liquor is generally too salty to use alone, but it's definitely guid for tattie or lentil soup.)

Smother the ham in butter and cover it entirely wi' foil. (A sloosh o' cider or aipple juice in the foil parcel is nice if ye hae it — keeps the ham nice and moist).

Bake in a slow oven, about thirty minutes to the pound, and when cooked, remove the foil, allow to get cold, and carve.

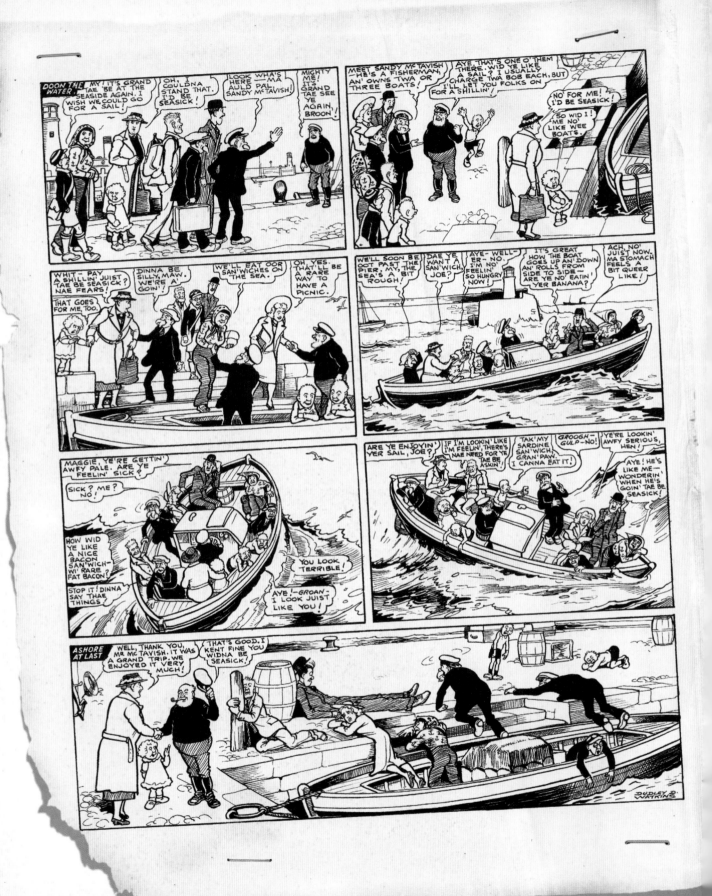

Horace's Index

St. Andrew's Ambulance Association

Class Certificate of Proficiency

This is to Certify

AMBULANCE WORK

...ded a Course of Instruction in

...passed a satisfactory examination in

...D TO THE INJURED.

Glasgo...

James...

No. 233813

ST. ANDREW'S · AMBULANCE · ASSOCIATION ·
INSTITUTED 1882
INCORPORATED BY ROYAL CHARTER 1899

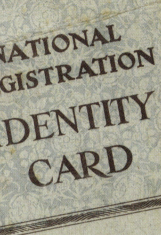

NATIONAL REGISTRATION

IDENTITY CARD

NEMO ME IMPUNE LACESSIT

SPECIAL COMPETITION—MANY PRIZES

HANDICRAFTS

VOL. 25   No. 383

THREEPENCE

FEBRUARY 1929

ARE YOU SATISFIED WITH YOUR WIRELESS CABINET?

IF NOT, SEE PAGE 53

OAK CABINET
Talled panel of any size up to 220 by 8ins.
Space below for batteries.

Automatic Cigarette Box

Hand Mirror

OTHER CONTENTS
HALL STAND
GRAMOPHONE RECORD
CABINET
WRITING DESK
COVERING A SCREEN
DOLL'S HOUSE FURNITURE
WOODWORKER'S A.B.C.
PUZZLES

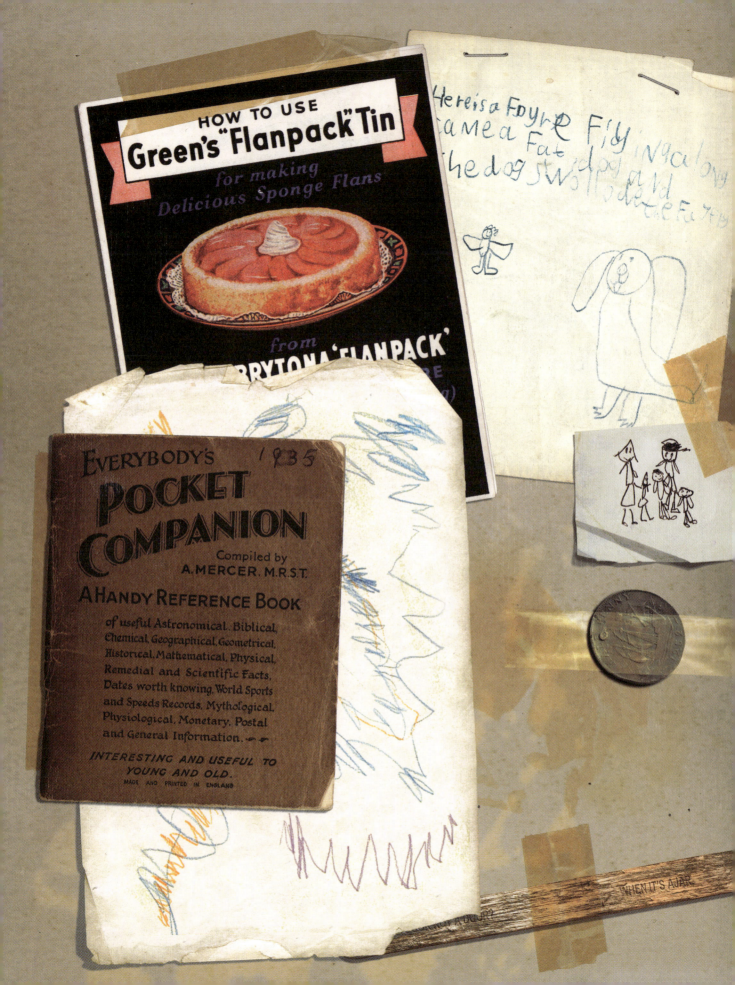